Brigadier General Samuel D. Rockenbach, Chief of Tank Corps
Photo courtesy of the National Archives at College Park, Maryland

Dale Street Books
Silver Spring, Maryland
Copyright © 2017 by Aleksandra M. Rohde
All rights reserved.

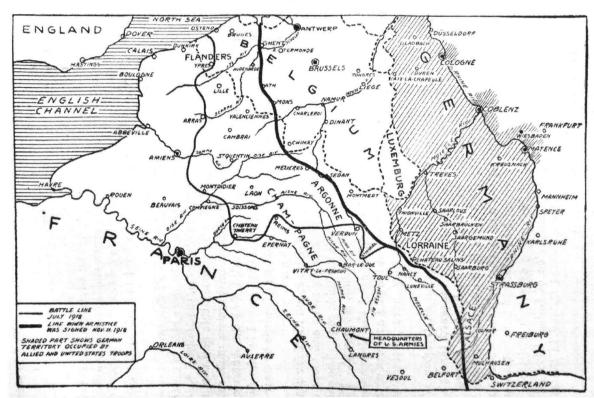

Battle Lines and Operations on the Western Front 1918, including German Territory held by the Allied Armies of Occupation. Source: Francis J. Reynolds, Allen L. Churchill, Francis Trevelyan Miller, Eds., The Story of the Great War, Vol. XV (P. F. Collier & Son: New York, 1920), p. 4513.

"Situation on August 20th, 1918. The American Tank Corps in France did not have a fighting Tank. It consisted of 600 trained personnel for light Tanks and 800 trained personnel for heavy Tanks. Twelve hundred men for heavy Tanks were training in England and 12 companies of light Tanks were enroute from the United States. In the United States we had 30 light Tank companies and 15 heavy Tank companies. The personnel carefully selected and the companies well trained as Infantry, machine gunners, truck drivers, and motor mechanics. They had never seen a Tank."

S.D. Rockenbach

TO THE READER

Operations of the Tank Corps A.E.F.[1] is the definitive treatise on the American Tank Corps in World War I, written by Brigadier General Samuel D. Rockenbach, its first commander. Commonly referred to as *"The Rockenbach Report,"* only a few typed copies are known to exist. It has never been published—until now. On the contrary, much has been published about one of Rockenbach's subordinate officers at the time, the famous World War II commander George S. Patton, Jr. But General Rockenbach is a much less familiar figure historically although he was hand-picked by General John J. Pershing to design, organize, man, train and deploy Tanks into 1918 France as part of the American Expeditionary Forces. Written in the same month as the Armistice was signed, General Rockenbach relates his experiences in developing and fielding this fearsome new combat arm, candidly citing the challenges as well as the victories.

Appended to the original—and included here—are supporting documents presented in their entirety. Significant portions of these documents are either paraphrased or directly quoted in the main body, i.e., the main narrative, of the *Report*. This is especially true in the chapters pertaining to operations at the Battle of St. Mihiel and in the Meuse-Argonne Offensive. But these are the unedited versions. They include the organization and manning list for the Tank Corps as of September 10, 1918, operations reports from the 304th (1st Provisional) Tank Brigade (commanded by George S. Patton, Jr.) and the 1st French Brigade on the Battle of St. Mihiel and the Meuse-Argonne Offensive. Also included is complete text of the operations report from the 301st American Tank Battalion, which had been allotted to the Australian Corps.

General Rockenbach also inserts within the main narrative verbatim transcriptions of other relevant documents, such as messages, general orders, plans, and memoranda. To help distinguish between the narrative and these

---

[1] Samuel D. Rockenbach, Operations of the Tank Corps A.E.F. with the 1st American Army at St. Mihiel and in the Argonne Sept. 11th to Nov. 11th 1918 and with the British E.F. Sept. 18th to November, 1918. (France: General HQs, A.E.F., Office of the Chief of Tank Corps, 1918). OCLC Number: 25526224, U.S. Army Heritage and Education Center, Ridgway Hall, Carlisle, Pennsylvania (D608 .R626 1918). Commonly referred to as *The Rockenbach Report*.

additional documents, a line is drawn in the text above and below the insertions and a different font used to further distinguish between the two.

Due in part to the different documents that were pulled together to form the original *Report*, as well as the supporting documents, each with its own writing style (and also because the original work was the product of military officers and not professional editors), there are inconsistencies throughout in capitalization usage, numbering conventions, formatting, etc., as well as grammar, spelling and punctuation errors. This necessitated minor corrections as well as stylistic adjustments for the sake of clarity (e.g., indentations, headings to distinguish between topics and subtopics, consistency in capitalization, and spelling out of some of the abbreviations).

For example, we capitalized the words "Tank" and "Infantry" throughout although they were capitalized in the original only by some writers and not by others. It also appears to have been the stylistic protocol in the Tank Corps A.E.F. to capitalize all the letters in names of geographic locations. This device for emphasizing relevant locations has been retained. Several lists were reformatted for ease of review and comparison, retaining the original data. These include two charts detailing the capabilities of the Mark VIII and Renault Tanks in the first chapter of the main narrative, "Introduction and History of the Tank Corps."

The original *Report*, written a century ago, has yellowed and faded with time, so we have carefully transcribed every word converting it to an easy-to-read format. A few words were so faded as to be indecipherable. If, despite our best efforts, we could not identify a word, we have duly footnoted it.

A different type of editorial challenge arises as a result of American soldiers struggling to spell the names of French villages, chateaus, ridges, trenches, rivers, etc. We have duly researched each name to confirm its correct spelling. But it is not always easy to tell if the name of a town, farm, road or salient was misspelled or more sadly if there were inadequate records at the time and it no longer exists. If the correct spelling of a point of interest could not be confirmed, it has been transcribed as it appears in the original text so as not to possibly exclude it from its rightful place in history. Where locations are written in French (e.g., "Bois," "Ferme" or "Saillant") the French is retained for this transcription (but without the accent marks). Where the report has

OPERATIONS OF THE TANK CORPS A.E.F.

Cover illustration from World War I recruiting poster.

By
Samuel D. Rockenbach

translated from the French into English in the original *Report*, the English version is transcribed (e.g., "Woods," "Farm" or "Salient,").

The accepted convention on numbering units—Roman numerals for corps level (e.g., V Corps rather than Fifth Corps or 5th Corps) and armies spelled out (First Army rather than 1st Army)—was not uniformly applied in the original. For clarity, the numbering format for corps and army level units has been edited to conform to convention within the main narrative. The supporting documents included at the end of the main narrative, however, have not been edited so that they can retain some of the individual look and feel of the multiple authors. Except for spelling and grammar corrections—or where added headings or adjusted formatting styles help to avoid ambiguity—these remain largely untouched.

Some images from the *Report* are inserted where they appear in the original text, including charts, diagrams, tables and a sampling of correspondence which hopefully help to convey a flavor of this seminal work. Unfortunately, while the original references a variety of photographs and maps supposedly attached to it, no photographs were found during our visits to the archives in Carlisle. One map was included with the original Report ("The Le Catelet-Bony Offensive") but it has faded significantly over time. Still it is included in this publication for its historic value. To provide context (especially with regard to geographic orientation), images of maps and photographs from other sources have been added to this publication. Where such images are inserted, they are appropriately notated as to their source.

We extend our heartfelt gratitude to the courteous and knowledgeable staff at the U.S. Army Heritage and Education Center, Ridgway Hall, in Carlisle, Pennsylvania for their tireless and companionable support during our longs hours of research. Throughout they remained cheerful, patient, and always eager to help. The Center and its splendid staff are a valuable resource not just to the Army, but to all who want to learn more of our country's rich military history. Special thanks to Elisabeth and Dave Glick and Kathy and Jacques Rigolage for their expert assistance navigating the French language, especially for the more obscure locations that would otherwise not have been properly identified.

<u>Operations of the Tank Corps A.E.F.</u> may be 100 years old, but it remains relevant in this increasingly volatile, technologically advancing, world. The challenge faced then—how to wage war even as new weapons of war are rushed into the battlespace without the luxury of time to fully test their strengths and weaknesses—remains a challenge and a cautionary tale for our leaders today. At the same time, it is a testament to American will and all that we can accomplish once we decide to act.

This is a story that needs to be told and more widely shared for the history General Rockenbach reveals and the wisdom he imparts. With this first-time publication, the *Rockenbach Report* has been rescued from the dark vaults of distant archives along with the man himself; so that more of us can learn about this singular American officer and the pivotal role he played in the Great War.

Aleksandra M. Rohde
11 November 2017

TABLE OF CONTENTS

TO THE READER 5

INTRODUCTION AND HISTORY OF THE TANK CORPS 11

    TANK FUNCTION, TYPES, TACTICS AND ORGANIZATION 16

        Function of Tanks 16

        Types of Tanks 16

        Tactics of Tanks 17

        Mark VIII Tank 17

        Renault (Light) Tank 20

        Training 21

        Organization 23

    SITUATION ON AUGUST 20TH, 1918 25

ST. MIHIEL TANK CORPS OPERATIONS 27

    PLANS FOR TANK OPERATIONS 29

    EXECUTION 34

        Schneider Tanks 34

        Brigade Reserve 35

        Artillery Preparation 35

        Operations September 13 - 16 35

    FRENCH TANK OPERATIONS 37

    GERMAN OFFICIAL REPORT 42

TANK OPERATIONS EAST OF MOSELLE 43

TANK OPERATIONS IN THE ARGONNE 45

    PLANS FOR TANK OPERATIONS 47

    OPERATIONS OF THE FIRST AMERICAN TANK BRIGADE 49

        Plans for Tank Operations 49

        Execution 50

Tactical Conclusions	58
OPERATIONS OF THE FRENCH TANKS	60
Plans for Tank Operations	60
Execution	62
Tactical Conclusions	69
General Conclusions	69
AMERICAN TANKS WITH THE BRITISH E.F.	71
301ST BATTALION	71
306TH REPAIR AND SALVAGE COMPANY	73
SUPPORTING DOCUMENTS	75
ORGANIZATION TANK CORPS 1ST ARMY	77
304TH AMERICAN BRIGADE AT ST. MIHIEL	83
1ST FRENCH BRIGADE AT ST. MIHIEL	95
1ST (304TH) AMERICAN BRIGADE AT MEUSE-ARGONNE	111
1ST FRENCH BRIGADE AT MEUSE-ARGONNE	129
301ST BATTALION WITH THE BRITISH EXPEDITIONARY FORCES	153
301ST LOSSES IN ACTION ON SEPTEMBER 29	175
PERSHING COMMENDATION	183

INTRODUCTION AND HISTORY OF THE TANK CORPS

"Prussia in the Field: Now superior upon the whole in tactics and superior in the tactical instruments (until the advent of the Tanks.)"[2]

At the Battle of the Somme, "then first appeared the new tactical instrument, the Tank, which was to have so great an effect upon the future of the war.

x x x x x x x x x x

The first of these two points upon which I am insisting—the appearance of numerical weakness upon the side of the enemy—the effect of continued attrition was achieved by the sacrifice of the English; by the very heavy expenditure of their new armies. The second feature, the Tank, was later to prove of even greater importance. For the first time a new tactical instrument had appeared, capable of dealing with the chief elements of the modern defensive, and though it had not yet appeared in sufficient numbers, nor even in a quite adequate form, there it was; a step had been taken in advance of the enemy which he never recovered. Fifteen months later we were to see the first example of what that new tactical instrument could do at its fullest efficiency; two years later it was to become a deciding factor.

x x x x x x x x x x

After the reduction of the Amiens salient, the end of August saw a further lighting up of the line to the north in front of Arras, and of Douai. The enemy lost his last elaborate defence and fell back in fear of the Tanks upon a water line just before Douai."

–Hilaire Belloc, December 19th and 26th, 1918, in LAND & WATER.

---

[2] First page of original *Report*. Rockenbach begins his *Report* by quoting a well-known writer and historian of the time.

GENERAL HEADQUARTERS
American Expeditionary Forces
Office of Chief of Tank Corps.

27 December, 1918.

OPERATIONS OF TANK CORPS A.E.F. AT ST. MIHIEL, in the MEUSE-ARGONNE OPERATION, and with the BRITISH E.F.

Although the Tank Corps participated in all the activities of the First Army from September 11th until the Armistice on November 11th, 1918, there are not many who had any personal experience with the Tanks used. Only one type, the light, was used. The conditions under which the Tanks operated were so contrary to plans and so unusual and abnormal that before forming any conclusions as to their value, you should get the American Expeditionary Forces idea as to Tanks and the proposed plan of employment. This can best be obtained by considering the conception and development of the Tank Corps and its size on August 20th, 1918.

Prior to the arrival of the A.E.F., the American Military Mission in Paris had, by direction of the Chief of the War College, investigated and submitted a report under date of May 21st, 1917, giving the latest British and French technical and tactical ideas on the use of Tanks. Major Frank Parker, Liaison Officer at G.H.Q. of the French Armies of the North and North-East, submitted notes covering French Tanks in the Allied Offensive of April, 1917. In the light of our recent experience his two chief criticisms are of interest:

"(a) Insufficient protection against fire. Little extinguishing material was provided.

(b) Faulty liaison with the Infantry. On several occasions the Tanks went ahead of the Infantry and were destroyed for lack of support. Many were destroyed."

The French at that time had only two types of Tanks; the St. Chaumond and the Schneider. Neither were Tanks in the sense of later development. They were more properly artillery carriers. They had to be preceded by a group of skirmishers who indicated the route for them to follow. They were bad cross-country machines; under powered; badly arranged and it was all off with the crews if they were stuck.

A joint British and French Tank Board met in London early in May, but were unable to reconcile their ideas as to machines or tactics. The British preferred the heavy Tank to be used in advance of the Infantry and the French desired their light Tank, which they were building, to be used in close liaison with the Infantry. Their normal position to be with the battalion support and only to advance when the Infantry was held up.

Shortly after the arrival of the Commander-in-Chief, of the A.E.F., and his staff in France in June, 1917, various committees were appointed and sent to the British and French fronts to study their organization plans and equipment. Naturally "Gattling Gun" (J.H.) Parker noted and reported on the counter to the machine gun. On July 19th, 1917, the Commander-in-Chief directed the detail of the Board of well selected officers to study the new French Tank (Renault).

On July 28th, the Chief Ordnance Officer of the A.E.F. requested to be informed as to the number of Tanks required in order that a definite request might be made on the War Department to expedite construction. Colonel Eltinge, General Staff, in addition to his other duties, was put in charge of Tank matters.

On September 14th, the following cablegram was sent to the War Department:

```
No. 159-S Paragraph 15 - for Chief of Ordnance. Careful
study French and British experience with Tanks completed
and will be forwarded by early mail. Project includes three
hundred fifty heavy Tanks of British Mark Six pattern;
twenty similar Tanks equipped for signal purposes; forty
similar Tanks for supply of gasoline and oil; one hundred
forty Tanks arranged to carry twenty-five soldiers or five
tons of supplies; fifty similar Tanks with upper platform
for field gun; total six hundred heavy Tanks. Also
following Renault Tanks; ten hundred thirty for fighting
purposes; one hundred thirty for supply; forty for signal
purposes; total twelve hundred Renault Tanks. Replacement
of Tanks requires fifteen per cent per month after arrival
here. Mark Six Tanks should be in proportion of one small
```

cannon and four machine guns and the female carries six machine guns. Renault Tanks should be in proportion of two to carry a machine gun to one to carry a six-pounder, or one carrying three-inch gun. Other material required for Tank organization includes: three hundred six-ton auto trucks each carrying complete Renault Tank; ninety three-ton auto trucks; two hundred seventy three-ton auto trucks with trailers; ninety three-ton auto trucks with kitchen trailers; ninety Ford automobiles and one hundred eighty motorcycles. Understand that arrangements can be made with Renault Works to permit manufacture of Renault Tanks in United States and that they will furnish model. Also that complete plans and specifications for British Mark Six can be obtained. These are the only models of Tanks whose use is recommended by either British or French. British Mark Six is thirty feet long and weighs about thirty tons. It is a powerful machine but limited to particular localities. Groups are assigned to particular areas for fighting. Renault is about nine feet long and weighs about six tons. It is used in conjunction with Infantry and assigned to Infantry units. Arrangements for manufacture should be made at once. Understand that French desire about two thousand Renault Tanks from United States. Will take up with French War Office later. Tanks are used in large numbers or not at all, hence shipment not expected before next Spring. Will submit recommendations regarding organization later.

Pershing.

Project for Overseas Tank Corps based on 20 combat divisions, consisting of the necessary headquarters, five heavy and 20 light battalions employing 375 heavy and 1500 light fighting Tanks, was approved by the Commander-in-Chief, A.E.F. on September 23rd and sent to the War Department. Details were to be worked out and submitted later.

On October 14th Majors Drain and Alden of the Ordnance Department were detailed by Special Order, H.A.E.F. with instruction from the Chief Ordnance Officer, A.E.F., to collect all information obtainable on the use, design, and production of Tanks. Their report, submitted on November 10th, was exhausting and interesting.

In order to coordinate the production efforts, an Inter-Allied Tank Commission was approved and Major Drain was appointed the American member thereof. He was directed to proceed in the attempt to get an agreement with the British and French as to the best type of Tank to be constructed and coordinate the production effort so as to get the largest number of Tanks in the minimum time. The effort with the British was a success and the Anglo-American Commission decided the type of heavy Tank, which was nothing more in idea than an enlarged Renault, and started design. The French, while approving, would take no active part. On December 6th the American member of the Supreme War Council, with the approval of the Commander-in-Chief A.E.F., cabled the War Department and got approval to enter into an Inter-Allied agreement for the joint production of 1500 of the Liberty Mark VIII Tanks, and for the allotment of 1500 Liberty engines for the same. The 1500 heavy Tanks were to be produced by the 1st of October, 1918.

In the meantime, Captain G. S. Patton, Jr., Cavalry,[3] and Lieutenant Elgin Braine, had been on duty with the French Tanks. They had thoroughly mastered the light Tank (chars d'assaut Renault). They were very enthusiastic about it and were ready to make improvements. The War Department was cabled, requesting the rapid construction of the Renault Tanks. Steps were taken to secure and send specifications and two Renault Tanks to the United States. As the Renault is manufactured by a private concern, the negotiations were slow and tedious.

Doubts as to the usefulness of Tanks were removed by the Battle of Cambrai, starting on the 20th of November, 1917. The salient points brought out as to the value of Tanks were: Economy in men per weapon, in men per yard of front, in casualties, increased enemy's casualties, economy in Artillery personnel, in Cavalry personnel, in ammunition and manufacture, of transportation, of labor on the battlefield, of property, of tonnage and of time.

---

[3] Patton was promoted in quick succession in early 1918. He had been wearing his Major clusters for only a week before he was notified that he was promoted to Lieutenant Colonel in April 1918. Stanley P. Hirshson, "General Patton: A Soldier's Life," (New York: Perennial, 2003), p. 115.

At Cambrai a penetration of 10,000 from a base of 12,000 yards was made in 12 hours. That the Boche counterattack left the British in worse situation than before the attack in no way diminished the usefulness of Tanks, but made clear that Tanks were not an independent arm. There must always be the Infantry to support the Tanks and secure their gains. (Cambrai was a strategical success in that it held troops away from Italy).

This was the situation on December 23rd when I arrived at G.H.Q. and was detailed as Chief of Tank Corps.

Tank Function, Types, Tactics and Organization

Instructions were to decide at once on the types of Tank, the number necessary, the organization necessary to fight them under the approved project of September 23rd, and be ready to fight as soon as possible. All the data available was gone over. All sections of the General Staff and Service Departments had all they could do and could give no help. It was necessary to decide what was the probable maximum amount we could chew and not bite off any more. Decision was made first as to the function of Tanks. They might have universal application in war, but the following was laid down as a basis for all subsequent effort:

Function of Tanks

The function of Tanks is to assist the Infantry by making a path for it through the wire and protect it from destructive loss from machine gun and rifle fire.

Types of Tanks

Taking Mr. Ford as authority on production, it was out of the question that we could produce the numerous types in production by the British and French, nor even those stated in our cablegram of September 14th. Hence it was decided to confine ourselves to fighting Tanks and to restrict the types to two: a heavy and a light. The best British heavy Tank at that time, the Mark IV, has been aptly described as a deaf, dumb, and blind beast. An improvement had to be made on that, and as far as we could get any consensus of opinion, the Liberty or Mark VIII would possess all the qualities that the fighting man requires. The United States could not manufacture guns and armor plate in time to be of any use. If we got heavy Tanks, it would have to be an Anglo-American machine.

For the light Tank, the French Renault was decided on, but with a number of essential improvements. It was to have a bulkhead separating the gun room from the engine so that the crew could not be burned to death; was to have a self-starter; was to have its gasoline Tank double cased with an inch of felt lining between, so that when penetrated by a bullet there would be no leakage of gas; and to have an interchangeable mount so that the same Tank could carry either a machine gun or a 37mm gun.

For the trucks, trailers and tractors necessary for transporting and supplying Tanks, it was decided to take commercial machines or those already in production. As to the number of Tanks, we were limited to the equipment provided in the project of September 23rd: 375 heavy fighting Tanks and 1500 light fighting Tanks with 15% per month replacement.

Tactics of Tanks

As to tactics for Tanks, Tanks were to conform to the tactics of Infantry. They were an auxiliary arm and must conform.

Organization. It was evident that if we were going to win the war, we would have to take the offensive for prolonged periods. The Tank organization of our Allies did not permit carrying on a continuous fight for weeks (it was not expected to carry on a continuous fight for months, as our recent experience showed necessary). Tanks must have an organization providing reliefs so that the crews that fought today would not be required to fight tomorrow, and back of the companies, battalions and brigades there must be trained feeder companies able to replace disabled men within 12 hours.

Mark VIII Tank

A meeting was held in Paris on the 26th of December with the Chief Ordnance Officer, A.E.F., and the American Tank Commissioner. The Mark VIII or Liberty Tank was formally approved and steps taken to speed up completion of design and working drawings. The Liberty or Mark VIII was to be a joint production by the British and United States, 50% of the components to be furnished by each nation, and the Tanks were to be assembled at NEUVY-PAILLOUX near CHATEAUROUX. This Tank was to be built and delivered entirely by the Anglo-American Commission. This was confirmed by a Treaty Agreement between Great Britain and the United States signed in London on January 22nd.

Deliveries were to begin in July and schedule completed by the 1st of October. The failure of the Aviation program prevented us getting the engines and the March offensive of the Boche prevented the British producing their components.

Mark VIII Tank. Source:
https://commons.wikimedia.org/wiki/File:Allied_Mark_VIII_(Liberty)_Tank.jpg.

Mark VIII

Weight	35 tons
Length	33 feet
Width	12 feet
Height	9 feet 10 inches
Speed	Maximum 6 miles per hour. Power 10 h.p. per ton of weight

- Flotation: 4.5 pounds per square inch. Any ground that will support a man
- Trench crossing ability: 14 feet
- Ability to climb vertical bank: 5 feet
- Armor proof against all small arm bullets, including armor-piercing
- Armament: 7 machine guns of which 6 can be fired at once. 2 six pounders
- Communication – Every Tank carries two pigeons and signal flags. Every 16th Tank has a radio set. Every Company has messengers.
- Cargo – 16 Infantry or machine gunners in addition to crew, or cargo, of two tons
- Wire – No obstacle
- Radius of action on one fill – 50 miles
- Mud – 18 inches of mud no obstacle
- Obstacles – Forests; stumps; boulders; shelled areas, soaked with water; and Tank pits
- Transport – By rail or cross country

Renault (Light) Tank

The Renault Works were visited with French officials and the designs of the Renault Tank and two Tanks were gotten off to the United States. By cable from the United States on the 2nd of February, 1918, the estimate of deliveries of the American built Renault were as follows: 100 in April, 300 in May and 600 monthly thereafter until completed. On November 11th, the date of the Armistice, no Tanks had been received from America by the Tank Corps. Two were received on November 20th.

American troops in the Forest of Argonne, 26 September 1918.
Source: National Archives and Records Administration, ARC 530748.

Renault

Weight	6 to 7 tons
Length	13.5 feet
Width	5 feet 7 inches
Height	7 feet
Speed	6 miles per hour

- Flotation: 5 pounds per square inch. 18 inches of mud no obstacle. Can cross any country an Infantryman [can]
- Trench crossing ability: 6 feet
- Climbing Ability: 2 feet 6 inches (doubled when coupled) 30 degree slope
- Armor proof against all small arm bullets
- Armament: 1 machine gun or 1 37 mm. Gun; Light Tanks operate in platoons of 5; 3 armed with Machine Guns and 2 with 37 mm. Guns
- Communication – Every Tank carries two pigeons and signal flags. Every 16th Tank is a radio Tank.
- Wire – No obstacle
- Radius of action – 25 miles on one fill
- Obstacles – Forests, stumps, boulders, shelled areas, soaked with water, and Tank pits
- Transport – By rail, truck, trailer, or cross country

Training

The great French Tank Training and Manoeuver Camp at COMPIEGNE was then visited. Night manoeuver demonstrated that Tanks could not be operated at night.

The British front was then visited and manoeuvers gone through with the British Tanks in No Man's Land to the east of Arras which were convincing as to the serious defects of the best British Tanks then in use. Then to the British Training Center at MERLIMONT and to the great central repair shop, where the best information as to defects, was available from broken parts and then to the British Home Training Center at WOOL, ENGLAND, where permission was obtained for establishing an annex training center for American officers and noncommissioned officers for instructors, heavy battalion, and a nucleus battalion, an aggregate of 1200, to the 1st of November.

Returning to G.H.Q., approval was obtained to use the British Training Center in England for the training of heavy Tank personnel and for establishing a training center for light Tanks at BOURG. BOURG was especially desirable, as the Tank training group was on the south edge of the A.E.F. Service Schools and we could [organize] for manoeuvers and training with officers and troops there, and in addition start an A.E.F. Tank School, as a branch of the Army Schools. Twenty-five Renault Tanks were obtained from the French for training.

Washington was cabled requesting that 50 selected officers and 100 noncommissioned officers be sent to England at once to be followed by a heavy battalion the first of March and one the first of each subsequent month until five battalions had been shipped.

Authority was given to accept transfers from other organizations in the A.E.F. to the number of 600 for the light Tanks. The United States was requested to select and organize the remaining companies and informed that instructors would be sent as soon as trained for the establishment of the training center in the United States.

In order to remove the idea that has been expressed by some that you could put a truck driver in the driver's seat of the Tank, and a machine or 37mm gunner in the gun room and handle a Tank, it is asked that you keep in mind that a Tank is a land cruiser and they cannot be handled without a most diligent pursuit by intelligent men of the following courses of Instruction and Training:

Infantry. An intensive course in Infantry training to include the school of the company, 30 days. This course to include signaling, visual training, pigeons, gas and pistol

> (a) Mechanical: gas engines, mechanical construction of large and small Tanks – 5 days

(b) Tank Drivers – 4 days
(c) 6 Pdr. Gun – 9 days
(d) 37mm Guns – 9 days
(e) Machine Gun – 9 days
(f) Compass so that man can manoeuver his Tank with apertures closed – 4 days
(g) Signal – 6 days
(h) Visual Training: Training to recognize and identify various features of the enemy's battle area – 2 days
(i) Pigeons – 1 day
(j) Gas – 1 day
(k) Intelligence – 30 days

Officers of a Tank company and battalion commanders required a minimum of 57 days training. Reconnaissance officers - 44 days. Noncommissioned officers to take charge of a light Tank – 61 days. All other officers – 57 days. The training varied from a minimum of three months to six months.

Organization

A revised project for combat Tank Corps was approved by G.H.Q., A.E.F., on February 18th, and Washington on the 21st of March. This gave us the necessary headquarters, five battalions of heavy and 20 light, repair and salvage companies, depot companies, training centers and replacement companies in France equal to 25% of the combat forces and in the United States 25% more.

By July the importance of Tanks had increased and an increase of five heavy battalions was authorized to be organized with the previously authorized battalions into 10 brigades, each consisting of a headquarters, one heavy battalion, two light battalions, repair and salvage company. All Tank Corps troops were to be G.H.Q. troops and to be allotted to armies according to the theatre and nature of the operation. For the three armies contemplated, a combat force for only two was allowed. Allotment for an Army was to consist, normally, of an Army Tank Corps headquarters with a Heavy Artillery

Ordnance Mobile Repair Shop and five brigades. Each Army group was to be based on a training center. This would give us a total of 750 heavy fighting Tanks, 1450 light fighting Tanks, with a reserve of 15% per month.

Summary of Organization

Personnel	21,800
Heavy Tanks	730
Light Tanks	1,520
Guns, 6-pdr. 1460, batteries	365
Guns, 37mm. 600, batteries	150
Guns, machine, 6680, companies	557

The personnel and equipment was designed to carry on a continuous fight. Tanks are not to fight for two or three days and then retire for repairs, but disabled Tanks and crews would be replaced from the support and reserve. The damaged Tanks being repaired where possible by the brigade repair and salvage company in the field.

Tank brigades were to be stationed in division areas where they would train and manoeuver with the divisions that they were likely to operate with.

In April 1918, the Inter-Allied Tank Committee, consisting of the Chief of the French, British, Italian and American Tank Corps, was formed, met at VERSAILLES on the 1st day of May and monthly thereafter. The object of this Committee was to keep abreast on mechanical and tactical improvements, to keep coordinated the effort for production and for the Americans to secure the necessary shipping. Through this Committee, in June, it being evident that we could get no useful number of Tanks from America before 1919, we were able to get a promise from the French to equip two American battalions with light Tanks, and from the British to equip the battalion that had completed its training in England, with heavy Tanks, provided it was attached to the British in France for operation.

SITUATION ON AUGUST 20TH, 1918

The American Tank Corps in France did not have a fighting Tank. It consisted of 600 trained personnel for light Tanks and 800 trained personnel for heavy Tanks. Twelve hundred men for heavy Tanks were training in England and 12 companies of light Tanks were enroute from the United States.

In the United States we had 30 light Tank companies and 15 heavy Tank companies. The personnel carefully selected and the companies well trained as Infantry, machine gunners, truck drivers, and motor mechanics. They had never seen a Tank.

ST. MIHIEL TANK CORPS OPERATIONS

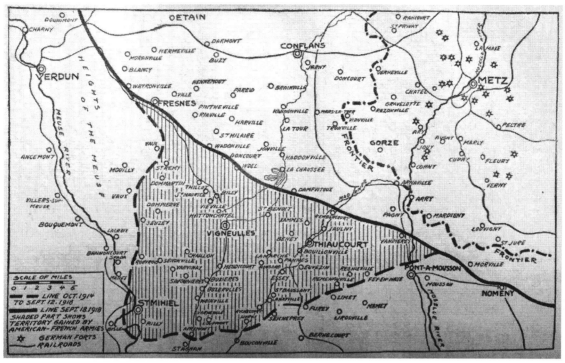

"*The Victory of the American Army at St. Mihiel.*"
Source: Francis J. Reynolds, Allen L. Churchill, Francis Trevelyan Miller, Eds.
<u>The Story of the Great War</u>, Vol. XV (P.F. Collier & Son: New York, 1920), p. 4691.

On August 18th, 1918, two orders were received by the Chief of Tank Corps, A.E.F.: One to proceed to PARIS for consultation with the Assistant Secretary of War as to securing Tanks from the British and French, and the other to report to the Chief of Staff, First Army, at NEUFCHATEAU, for temporary duty.

In Paris every available resource of the American Government was used to aid in a quick supply of Tanks. The mechanical officer of the Tank Corps and the five assistant officers were ordered to the French factories to see that the Tanks were loaded and then to accompany them to the Tank Center at BOURG.

Reporting to Headquarters, First Army on the 20th of August, the original general plan for the reduction of the ST. MIHIEL SALIENT was given and information that we would have three battalions, 150 British heavy Tanks, three battalions 225 French light Tanks, and the two American battalions would be equipped with 144 French light Tanks. It was emphasized that the higher command had pointed out that the salient could not be reduced without too great a loss of life unless heavy Tanks were employed to break through the maze of wire that surrounded the salient.

From personal reconnaissance made in January and February and map studies of the terrain, only a very limited use of Tanks was possible. The trenches were too wide and crumbling to permit the crossing of the light Tanks, unless preceded by heavies, or assisted by Pioneers. In much of the area the water was close to the surface and very little rain would produce bogs. The RUPT DE MAD was an impassable obstacle at all times unless the bridges were intact.

On the 20th of August the 1st American Tank Corps Brigade was attached to the First Army for temporary duty and directed to report to the Chief of Tank Corps, First Army, when equipped for action.

The commander of the brigade with his staff was directed to report at once and on arrival was sent to report to the Commanding General, the V Corps, for reconnoitering his front with a view to employing Tanks. On the 15th of August, the Chief of Staff, Tank Corps, due to fear that he would never get into the fight if he waited for Tanks, had been released and was on duty with the 2nd Engineers. He was ordered to report, a staff was selected from the Tank Center, and the Headquarters of the 3rd Brigade was organized. This Headquarters was ordered to report to the Commanding General, the IV Corps, for the purpose of reconnoitering his front with a view to employing Tanks. Tank Corps Headquarters was established at LIGNY-EN-BARROIS.

Telegraphic request was made for the British and French brigade commanders with their staffs to report at once.

On August 25th, definite information had been received that no heavy Tanks could be furnished by the British. This meant no machines capable of reaching the wire ahead of the Infantry, the loss of 300 6-pounder guns (75 batteries) and 600 machine guns covering the advance. The rate of equipping the American battalions indicated only one would be ready on the 1st of September. Definite information could not be obtained from the French as to what they would furnish.

Plan was submitted, based on "if's," and attempt made to explain why the light Tank could not reach wire on the other side of trenches over six feet wide as the heavy Tank could, and that while it could break down and bury wire, it could not get to most of that on our front and that it could not lead the Infantry and would have to be assisted by Pioneers. Nothing in the plan of attack should be based on light Tanks. Request was made to reduce the artillery preparation. A 31-hour shelling would make the terrain impracticable for Tanks.

The 27th of August the situation was unchanged, except that we were sure that two American battalions would be equipped by the 1st of September and could be fought by the 5th, if circumstances were most favorable. Lieutenant Colonel Wahl, Commandant of the 1st Brigade, d'A.S., with his staff was ordered to report to the Chief of Tank Corps, A.E.F. His command was to consist of four battalions of French light Tanks.

Daily, the fact was emphasized that the Tanks available could not do what the original plan contemplated.

PLANS FOR TANK OPERATIONS

The 30th of August the following plan was submitted:

```
          HEADQUARTERS - TANK CORPS - FIRST ARMY
                                              30 Aug 18
From: Chief of Tank Corps, First Army
To: Chief of Staff, 1st Army
Subject: Plan for employed T. C. Troops
     1. Based on detailed reconnaissance and the information
that the French will furnish us four battalions of light Tanks
(300 machines) and that our First Brigade, two battalions (144
machines), will be ready the 1st of September, the following
plan is submitted - Allotment:
     Two French battalions to I Corps, to ease the way for the
Infantry on the sector FEY-EN-HAYE-LIMEY.
     Two French battalions to the IV Corps, for the sector LIMEY
(exclusive)-RICHECOURT.
```

Liaison will be secured by the C. S. Tank Corps acting with Colonel Wahl, Commander of the French Tank Brigade.

American Brigade (two battalions) to V Corps to ease the way for the Infantry on the sector HAUDIMONT-BONZEE.[4]

2. The Headquarters Tank Brigade is established with the V Corps for the western sector and with the IV Corps for the eastern sector. Detraining points for the eastern sector ANSAUVILLE; for the western sector SOMMEDIEUE.

3. CONCENTRATION. Request has been made to G.H.Q. to give the necessary orders to insure the railway transport department getting notice to provide equipment at H-144, to start the movement at H-120, so as to assure the arrival of units for I and IV Corps at detraining point at H-78 and for the IV Corps at H-54.

To carry this out it is requested that a R.R.T.O. at U.S.P.O. 714, be directed to get in touch with the commanding officer, 311th T.C. at that point, and another to report to Lieutenant Colonel Pullen, C.S.T.C., at ECROUVES, (4 kilometers west of TOUL) and another to report to Lieutenant Colonel Patton, at Headquarters V Corps. The last two will be needed at H-80.

S. D. ROCKENBACH,
Brigadier General,
U.S.A.

On September 1st the main supply dump for Tanks operating on the south face of the salient was established at ECROUVES. This, while too small to remain in the minds of G-4, First Army, contained 20,000 gallons of gasoline, 2000 gallons of light automobile oil, 600 gallons of heavy automobile oil, and 600 pounds of grease. On the 1st, 2nd and 3rd of September, manoeuvers of one battalion of French light Tanks were held near COLOMBEY-LES-BELLES at which quite a number of officers of the divisions were present.

---

[4] Alternatively Haudimont is spelled "Haudiomont" in the "304th American Brigade at St. Mihiel," found in the supporting documents.

The 3rd of September, due to the modification of the general plan, the 1st American Tank Brigade was relieved from the V Corps and attached to the IV Corps. Definite information was received as to what the French were to furnish. To overcome the lack of the British heavy Tanks, we were camouflaged with a few St. Chaumond and Schneider Tanks, neither of which was capable of preceding the Infantry without assistance. Both types were to be discarded as soon as they could be replaced.

By the 5th of September all reconnaissance had been completed. Dams were prepared for the RUPT DE MAD near BOUCONVILLE, so that it could not rise in case of rain. Material was gotten ready to repair quickly the bridges that must be used. Another alternative was to attempt to head the RUPT DE MAD with a company and rush the north bank.

On September 11th, warning was received from the Commander-in-Chief of the French Tank Corps that the Tanks with which we were equipped should not be employed in action until they had been operated 12 days. In the afternoon, another warning was received, that due to the rain, Tanks would not be able to operate as planned. Reply was made to this that as long as we did not have over two inches of mud, it would act as a lubricant and we would operate. The general plan was as follows:

HEADQUARTERS FIRST ARMY
AMERICAN EXPEDITIONARY FORCES, FRANCE

ANNEX No. 3.   5 Sept 18
FIELD ORDERS No. 9.

PLAN OF EMPLOYMENT OF TANKS

1. Based on the general plan, detailed reconnaissances, and the troops to be available, viz., one Regiment French light Tanks; (one groupement and two groups, French medium Tanks; 1st American Brigade (two battalions light Tanks) and Headquarters, 3rd American Brigade; the following allotment of Tanks is made:

(a) **ALLOTMENT**:

(1) The 505th French Regiment (three battalions) and one Groupement, to the I Corps.

Liaison with the Corps to be maintained by the Chief of Staff, Tank Corps, and Headquarters 3rd American Brigade.

Detraining points: BOIS VILLERS-EN-HAYE, BOIS DE LA RAPPE.[5]
 (2) The 1st American Brigade (two battalions) and two French Groups to the IV Corps.
 Detraining point: ANSAUVILLE.
 (b) Headquarters Tank Corps Troops at ECROUVES.

Official:
By command of General Pershing:
S. D. ROCKENBACH,   H. A. DRUM,
Brigadier General, U.S.A.   Chief of Staff.
Chief of Tank Corps

The detraining plan was arranged in conjunction with the Chief of Railway Artillery so as to detrain in three nights at ANSAUVILLE, BOIS VILLERS-EN-HAYE and BOIS DE LA RAPPE. Provision was made for the last unit to detrain at H-48. We succeeded at H-2. Following is the order of detraining:

HEADQUARTERS - TANK CORPS - FIRST ARMY

6 Sept 18

From: Chief of Tank Corps, First Army
To: Chief of Staff, First Army
Subject: Detraining Table

 1. Below is complete plan for detraining Tank Corps units in three nights. Investigation of the railway situation and detraining points makes this appear to be a much more desirable schedule than attempting it in two nights, and if the necessary instructions are given to all concerned to cooperate in it, it will assure the arrival of the units at their destination at the proper time and with the minimum amount of interference with regard to railway traffic:

---

[5] Referred to elsewhere in this Report by its English translation, "Rappe Woods."

	Total Trains	H-104 A	V	R	H-80 A	V	R	H-56 A	V	R
2 Am. Bns.	4				2			2		
1 Reg. French	6		2			2			2	
1 Groupement St. Chaumond	2			1			1			
1 Group Schneider and Renault	2	2								
TOTALS	14	2	2	1	2	2	1	2	2	

NOTE: A- Ansauville; V- Bois Villers-en-Haye; R- Bois de la Rappe.

Image from archived Report.

2. The important consideration in the above schedule is that the 3rd Battalion of the French Regiment to move to destination at H-56 above, should arrive at PUNEROT (south of COLOMBEY-LES-BELLES) today, where it will be used for training.

Instructions should be given so as to assure railway equipment of this battalion being at RUPPES at H-64. (Equipment for the 2nd Battalion, detraining at H-80 might be held for this purpose.

Copy to: G-3 and G-4

S. D. Rockenbach,
Brigadier General, U.S.A.

The plan for the employment of Tanks was based on much careful and detailed study. That decided, the Army plan should contain nothing but the allotment of Tank organizations to the Corps Tank brigade commanders with this [sic] then went over the Corps plan, submitted their estimate as to what Tanks could do and on this combined study the Corps assigned Tanks to the divisions and the divisions to the brigades.

The Plan for the 1st American Brigade was as follows: the 14th and 17th Groups of French Schneiders (24 Tanks) and the 327th American Battalion (less 16 Tanks) were assigned to operate in the sector of the 42nd Division. Position of readiness south edge of BOIS DE LA HAZELLE; point of departure on D-1 night; east edge of BOIS DE REMIERES.

The 326th Battalion was assigned to operate in the sector of the 1st Division.

Position of readiness: North and FAUX BOIS DE NAUGINSARD.
Position of departure of D-1 night: North XIVRAY-ET-MARVOISIN.

EXECUTION

On the 12th of September the 327th Battalion attacked between the eastern edge of BOIS DE REMIERES and western edge of BOIS DE LA SONNARD in the direction of ESSEY.

Owing to the difficult ground Tanks were unable to precede the Infantry until the TRANCHEE DES HOUBLONS had been passed. They were then if possible to precede the Infantry in the attack on ESSEY and PANNES. The width of the trenches, and soft banks, proved insurmountable difficulties for most of the Tanks. Two were put out of action by direct hits. The five leading Tanks of the battalion entered ESSEY with the Infantry, thence they took the lead on PANNES. Thence one proceeded on the road toward BENEY but was recalled as the Infantry was ordered to advance in the direction of the woods northeast of BENEY. In this operation they drove out machine guns and overran one battery of 77's.

Late in the afternoon the battalion rallied at PANNES for gas and oil.

Schneider Tanks

These Tanks were attached to the left, or 83rd Brigade in the 42nd Division. The 14th Company was allotted to the right regiment, 165th, and the 17th Company was allotted to the left regiment, the 166th. One section was allotted to each attacking battalion and one section to the regimental reserve in readiness position in the BOIS DE LA HAZELLE. Owing to the width and conditions of the trenches the Schneiders were unable to precede the Infantry but followed the first wave closely as far as MAIZERAIS and were then halted in accordance with orders. While approaching MAIZERAIS one Tank was struck with a 150 shell and 15 men killed and wounded.

Operation of the 344th Battalion with the 1st Division: One platoon of this battalion attacked the SAILLANT DU HAREM east of the RUPT DE MAD and succeeded in getting the wire cut in front of this salient in advance of the Infantry. The remaining Tanks, operating to the west of the river, moved between RICHECOURT in the direction of LAHAYVILLE and against the machine guns in the BOIS DE RATE. A good many of these Tanks were struck in the trenches, but 25 reached the town of NONSARD which they entered in advance of the Infantry, silencing machine guns and 77's along the east edge of the BOIS DE RATE and BOIS QUART DE RESERVE, rallied in the afternoon on the RUPT DE MAD at point 356.5-237.8.

Brigade Reserve

One platoon of five Tanks left the Infantry parallels of departure at H-hour in the vicinity of BOYAU DE LA VERRIERES – BEAUMONT and moved along the south point of SALIENT DE VERRIERES east of the river and the remainder of the reserve left the point of readiness at H plus 30 minutes and followed in the rear of the leading elements of the 344th Battalion.

Owing to the nature of the ground, Tanks used three times as much gasoline as had been calculated and they were all out of gas by 3:00 p.m. Gas was gotten up to them by sleds, but the gas in trucks which attempted to move on the FLIREY-ESSEY road were unable to reach ESSEY until the afternoon of September 13th, 1918.

Artillery Preparation

Great assistance was rendered by the Artillery, which thoroughly cooperated with the Tanks by firing smoke shells mixed in the barrage along the edge of woods and observation posts. The ridges, especially the two spurs east and west of MAIZERAIS were well screened by smoke. Batteries were detailed for fugitive targets, anti-Tank guns, and so on.

Operations September 13 - 16

<u>September 13:</u> Fifteen Tanks of the 327th Battalion and 22 Tanks of the 14th and 17th French Groups arrived south of ST. BENOIT by noon. Here they remained in position the remainder of the day. During the afternoon 15 Tanks of the 327th Battalion arrived at ST. BENOIT. The 326th Battalion was not able to get a refill of gas until 2:00 p.m. They then moved through NONSARD to VIGNEULLES where 50 Tanks arrived at 12 midnight.

September 14: As the Tanks of the 326th Battalion were unable to gain touch with the 1st Division, it was decided to move through ST. MAURICE on WOEL, expecting to find the position along the WOEL-ST. BENOIT ROAD. The Tanks arrived 2 kilometers west of WOEL where the commanding officer was informed that the Germans had been driven out of WOEL and that this town was held by a platoon of 20 French Infantrymen. A message was sent to the Commanding General, 1st Division, requesting instructions and an officers' patrol was sent into the woods to the south to attempt to regain touch with the 1st Division or some portion of the IV Corps. In the meantime supply trucks arrived, Tanks refilled and men fed. During this operation the truck train was attacked by hostile aeroplanes.

At 12 noon it was decided to send a patrol of three Tanks and five dismounted men to WOEL thence 2 kilometers along the road to ST. BENOIT. At 1:30 p.m. an officer in charge of this patrol reported the town clear of the enemy and they were returning. At 2:00 p.m. he was attacked just south of WOEL by a battalion of Infantry, a battery of 77's and at least eight machine guns. He sent a runner to the battalion, stating the situation and that he was attacking. Five Tanks were sent to his assistance and left at 5:00 p.m. These Tanks, unsupported by Infantry, attacked the enemy and drove them to JONVILLE, destroyed five machine guns and causing the enemy to abandon a battery of 77's. In attempting to attach these guns to the rear of the Tanks, two officers and four men were wounded and the attempt to carry off the guns abandoned. Tanks returned to the battalion, 2 kilometers west of WOEL. At this time the enemy started to register on the location of the Battalion with 150's and as it had been ascertained that it was two miles in front of our line, it was decided to withdraw to ST. MAURICE.

September 15: At 9:00 p.m. on September 14th all Tanks received orders to withdraw and concentrate in the BOIS DE LA HAZELLE. This was done successfully with the exception of three French and two American Tanks which were partially destroyed by direct hits. All movements were made at night. The concentration in the BOIS DE LA HAZELLE was completed on the night of September 16th.

Conclusions. Owing to the failure of the enemy to make any serious resistance, the full value of Tanks in this operation was not possible to demonstrate. The Tanks unquestionably gave great moral support to our troops and had a demoralizing effect on the enemy. In spite of the terrain, which was believed to be impassable for Tanks, the Tanks were in position to aid the Infantry and would have done so had such assistance been necessary. The great value of the ST. MIHIEL operation from the Tank point of view was that the personnel had gotten rid of nervousness and could be expected to settle down to business in subsequent operations. It was demonstrated that the safest place on a battlefield was in a Tank. The necessity for a distinctive guidon for Tank Corps units and trucks and a marker for the men was demonstrated and adopted. The method of supply was revised and proved satisfactory in the ARGONNE.

Losses. From the 12th to the 16th of September, the losses were four officers wounded (only one while in a Tank); men killed five, wounded 15 (only three while in a Tank). [Out of] 174 Tanks in action, 3 [sustained] direct hits, 43 were out of action due to being ditched or mechanical trouble. Number of Tanks fit for action September 16th – 131.

FRENCH TANK OPERATIONS

HEADQUARTERS FIRST ARMY CORPS, A.E.F.

8 Sept 18

TANK CORPS OPERATIONS
ST. MIHIEL
First Brigade, French A. d'A.

FIELD ORDERS
No. 49

ANNEX NO. 4
PLAN OF TANKS.

The assignment of Tanks to the Corps will be three battalions of light Tanks (consisting of 45 Tanks each) and 36 heavy Tanks.

One battalion of light Tanks will be assigned to the 2nd and 5th Divisions each, and one battalion of light Tanks will be held in Corps Reserve, under a representative of the Tank Corps. Reserve Tanks will be held close to the position of the initial deployment, with a view to quick replacement of disabled Tanks, and for special cases that may arise.

Heavy Tanks will be used to assist in cutting pathways through wire for Infantry advance, and for use in reduction of important strong points.

The light Tanks with the leading Infantry battalions will be normally held up with their rear units, prepared to assist advanced troops when called upon.

Reconnaissance for movement into position will be made by Tank Corps officers. Conferences will be held by the Tank Corps officers with battalion and company commanders designated by division commanders to lead the attack, with a view to insuring mutual understanding between the Tanks and Infantry as to their respective tasks and the procedure to be followed under heavy contingency that can be foreseen.

The French report of the operation on the 12th of September is as follows:

---

505 REGIMENT TANKS

12 Sept 18, 21 hours

Headquarters: Report from Chef de Battalion Mare, Commanding the Tanks of the 1st C.A.U.S., concerning the operations of September 12, 1918

DISTRIBUTION:

For the 12th of September, the Tank Units placed at the disposition of the 1st C.A.U.S., were distributed in the following manner:

TANKS ST. CHAUMOND:

34th Group, at the disposition of the 5th Division (10th Brigade).

35th Group, at the disposition of the 2nd Division (3rd Brigade).

RENAULT TANKS:

14th Battalion Light Tanks at the disposition of the 5th Division (10th Brigade).

13th Battalion Light Tanks, at the disposition of the 2nd Division (3rd Brigade).

15th Battalion Light Tanks, in reserve.

OPERATIONS:

ST. CHAUMOND TANKS:

34th Group (12 Tanks on the starting point at 2 h., RAVIN REGNEVILLE leaves the position with eight Tanks, the others remaining at the starting point on account of trouble.) Of the eight Tanks which attacked, six were halted in the mud in the German trenches. Two attained the Army objective. The latest information shows that there are eight Tanks in good condition assembled in BOIS DE SAULX.

35th Group (11 Tanks starting point 300 m. north of LIMEY. Ten Tanks available BOIS DE LA HAIVE L'EVEQUE. Two Tanks mired at their starting position.) No information concerning the others.

LIGHT TANKS:

13th Battalion (2nd Division U.S.) attacks with the 3rd Brigade. 337th Company attacks with the 9th Regiment. At the starting position three sections and three hauling Tanks.

338th Company 12 Tanks at starting position. The others disembarked in the afternoon will reach at a later date.

339th Company at starting position with all Tanks in good order.

(Reserved Company, Marine Brigade).

According to information received, there are many Tanks halted in the trenches—seven in BOIS DU FOUR—one fell in a trap.

337th Company assembles at BOIS DE HEICHE.

At the end of the day, 30 Tanks reported south of THIAUCOURT (not verified).

The 339th Company north of BOIS DU FOUR, in full strength. No exact information on the disponibility.

14th Battalion Light Tanks attacked with the 10th Brigade.

340th Company all Tanks minus three at the starting position.

START:

Big difficulties in crossing the trenches. Eight Tanks halted. At 13 h. 30, 14 Tanks at VIEVILLE.

341st Company – All Tanks in starting position.

Crossing the trenches, all Tanks halted but two which reached VIEVILLE.

342nd Company reversed. All Tanks available.

15th Battalion Light Tanks – reserve of the A.C.

At the end of the day the entire battalion in position and disponible at the northern edge of BOIS DU FOUR.

CASUALTIES REPORTED:

34th Group; one killed, one wounded.

MATERIAL AVAILABLE FOR THE X 13th:

13th B.L.T.	61
14th B.L.T.	33
15th B.L.T.	65
34th Group ST. CHAUMOND	8
35th Group ST. CHAUMOND	10
Total	177

La Chef de Battalion Mare

On the afternoon of the 12th, 16 light and two St. Chaumond reached the BOIS D'HEICHE, all the rest were ditched.

Enough Tanks were in place by the 13th, so that they could have resisted a serious counterattack. By the 14th practically all the Tanks were assembled in the rear edge of the BOIS D'HEICHE and THIAUCOURT.

Tanks were withdrawn on the evening of the 15th.

The following by Colonel Wahl, French Brigade Commander, is interesting:

TACTICAL CONCLUSIONS[6]

1. Transport, especially detrainment, left much to be desired. The rails were blocked with trains of heavy artillery which were badly constructed and sometimes gave way. Ballast trains added to the confusion. Certain units remained 72 hours on the way. Consequently loss of time was experienced in getting into touch and extreme fatigue caused to personnel.

---

[6] This paraphrases Wahl's report. For verbatim transcription, see "1st French Brigade at St. Mihiel," in the supporting documents.

2. Road policing is often inexistent and sometimes unintelligent. Petrol convoys, for example, were sometimes stopped under the pretext that only ammunition was allowed to pass.

3. With a view to keeping operations secret, units were brought up late. Plans of attack were communicated at the last moment and the verbal instructions which could be picked up in staff offices were given with great scantiness. This resulted in great difficulties being experienced in getting into touch with Infantry units and in a great measure of uncertainty about the higher commands intentions. Thus, doubtless with a view to keeping plans secret, Tank units were kept in the forward area when it had been decided to continue operations no further and it was very difficult to obtain their withdrawal.

4. The enemy offered but insignificant resistance, the Infantry advanced very quickly. The Tanks were not called upon to intervene in the taking of the first system. Had they had to do so, they would only have been able to function with very diminished means, moving over a rain-sodden country and one which was furrowed by four-year-old defensive organizations. On the other hand, from the 13th September, units were in a position to get into battle practically up to strength but enemy resistance was still very feeble and it would appear that the Infantry, anxious to keep the glory of success totally for themselves, showed a certain hesitation in calling for the intervention of Tanks.

German Official Report

BATTLE OF ST. MIHIEL
12th Sept 1918

At 1:52 p.m. the 5th Ldw.[7] Division reported that, according to a report of the Infantry Brigade on the Bocksberg, Pannes and Nonsard had been surrounded and captured by the enemy. Tanks co-operating with Infantry were advancing from Nonsard against Heudicourt.

* * * * *

It was imperative for the Mihiel group to check a further enemy advance in a northerly and northwesterly direction beyond the line Nonsard-Pannes-Bouillonville.

The Infantry advancing with Tanks from Nonsard in the direction of Heudicourt would, in the opinion of Corps Headquarters, meet with the resting battalion of the 65th Ldw. Infantry Regiment which had been sent in that direction with accompanying artillery. It would probably be sufficient to drive the enemy back to Nonsard. Other forces would have to be sent by the group to fill up the gaps and assure the flank between Nonsard and Beney.

* * * * *

The Gorz Group, in reply to an inquiry, reported at 2:10 p.m. that it had no information to offer concerning the situation around Nonsard and Pannes. Tanks had gained possession of Raulecourt and Rambucourt.

* * * * *

At 2:30 p.m. the Gorz Group reported that masses of Infantry with Tanks and Cavalry opposite Sector G1 in the woods south of Montsec were preparing to attack. The artillery fire of the 5th Ldw. Division was immediately directed upon that point.

---

[7] Ludendorff.

TANK OPERATIONS EAST OF MOSELLE

On the 15th of September 15 American Tanks were placed at the disposal of the IV Corps for operation east of the MOSELLE.

These Tanks took up several positions of readiness on the front on the night of 21/22 and 22/23 and then quietly withdrew to VERDUN and entrained for the ARGONNE.

Their object was to deceive the enemy as to our intentions and cause him to strengthen his forces east of the MOSELLE.

This operation was reported successful.

TANK OPERATIONS IN THE ARGONNE

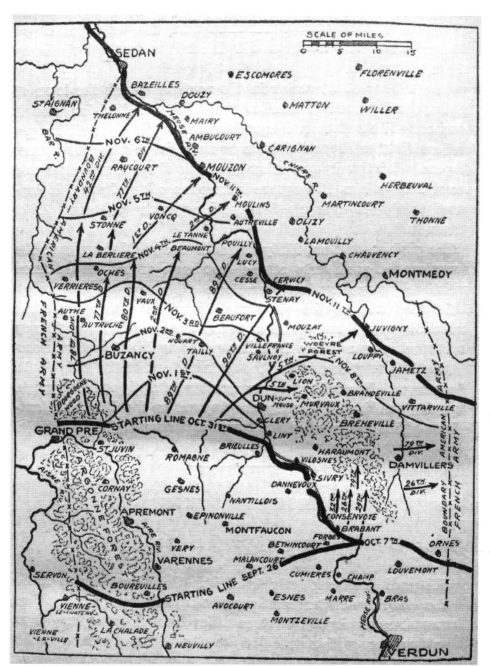

"The Meuse-Argonne Battle—September 26 to November 11, 1918."
Source: Francis J. Reynolds, Allen L. Churchill, Francis Trevelyan Miller, Eds.
The Story of the Great War, Vol. XV (P. F. Collier & Son: New York, 1920), p. 4766.

On September 4th I directed the Commander of the French Tank Brigade, as a matter of general interest, to secure photographs and have a senior officer reconnoiter the front then occupied by the French from the VERDUN-ETAIN ROAD to the east border of the ARGONNE. Reconnaissance was also started on the front for 20 miles east of the MOSELLE. Reports of these were made by the 10th. [A] map and following conclusions were made by the 14th:

1. The FORGES RIVER from the MEUSE to vicinity of MALANCOURT is an obstacle too great for Tanks, as are also the MALANCOURT, CHEPPY, and MONTFAUCON WOODS. For from 4 to 5 kilometers in rear of the enemy's front line the country is so covered with shell craters that its crossing by Tanks is extremely questionable. Hence Tanks can only be counted on to operate north of GERCOURT-CUISY-VERY-BAULNY line.

2. North of this line three sections offer favorable terrain for Tanks:
(a) One opening running south north, 1 kilometer wide at SEPTSARGES and expanding to 5 kilometers north of NANTILLOIS.
(b) One running southwest - northeast, west of MONTFAUCON and the ANDON RIVER (1000-1500 meters) wide.
(c) One zone bounded by the BUANTHE, the AIRE, the EXERMONT (rivulet) and the CHARPENTRY-ROMAGNE Road.

From this the following plan was prepared and submitted and approved with the addition in regard to assisting the III Corps.

Plans for Tank Operations

HEADQUARTERS FIRST ARMY
AMERICAN EXPEDITIONARY FORCES, FRANCE

17 SEPT 18

ANNEX No. 3
TO FIELD ORDER NO___ 1st American Army.

<u>PLAN FOR EMPLOYMENT OF TANK CORPS TROOPS</u>

1. The following is the general plan for the employment of Tanks:

(a) OPERATION. Tanks to assemble at the FORET DE HESSE. On D-Day they will follow the Infantry as soon as the way has been made passable for them, to their position of readiness in the BOIS DE MONTFAUCON and near CHEPPY. Thence they will operate in the sectors NANTILLOIS, MONTFAUCON, GESNES, and BAULNY-EXERMONT. On the HINDENBURG LINE being made passable for them, they should be in the best possible position for exercising their proper functions and will proceed to destroy machine gun nests, strong points, and to exploit the success.

(b) ALLOTMENT. The 505th Regiment, A.S. light and two groups St. Chamond to the Center (V) Corps to operate in the sectors of the right and center divisions north of the line GERCOURT-CUISY-VERY. The units assigned to the right division will wherever practicable assist the advance of the III Corps.

Detraining point DOMBASLE. Initial supply dump DOMBASLE.

The 504th Regiment (less one battalion) A.S. light, and one group St. Chamond to the center (V) Corps to operate in the sector of its left division north of the line CUISY-VERY. Detraining point DOMBASLE-EN-ARGONNE. Initial supply dump DOMBASLE.

The commanding officer and Headquarters, 3rd American Brigade to the Center (V) Corps for reconnaissance work and liaison of the French units attached to the Corps.

The 1st American Brigade, Group Schneider attached, to the left (I) Corps to operate in the sector of its right division north of BAULNY.

Detraining point RECICOURT. Initial supply dump RECICOURT.

  (c) TROOPS NECESSARY TO BE ATTACHED. One company of Pioneers to the units operating with the center (V) Corps. Two platoons Pioneers to the units operating with the left (I) Corps.
  (d) SUPPLY. The Corps to which Tank troops are attached will make necessary arrangements to insure gas and oil reaching them.
  (2) Headquarters Tank Corps at advanced section Army Headquarters.

OFFICIAL:
By command of General Pershing:
S. D. Rockenbach,   H. A. DRUM,
Brigadier General, U.S.A.   Chief of Staff.
Chief of Tank Corps

On September 16th the 1st American Tank Brigade was relieved from duty with the IV Corps, the Headquarters 3rd American Brigade and the 1st French Brigade from duty with the I Corps, and directed to report to Chief of Tank Corps, First Army.

 The general plan for the operation was gone over with the brigade commanders.

 The brigade commanders and staffs were directed to leave orders for the entraining of their commands and to proceed to reconnoiter the front of the center Corps and right division of the left Corps:

 The following supplies were called for:

...for the French Tank Corps units operating with the First Army at DOMBASLE at the earliest practicable date, same to be turned over to a French officer of the A.S.

```
        Liters gasoline                 325,000
        Liters fine oil                  32,000
        Liters Valvoline                 13,000
        Kilos grease                      6,000
        Liters ordinary oil               9,000
```

This should be placed, if convenient, in three lots, each lot to contain one-third of the above.

For the 1st Brigade American at RECICOURT, to be turned over to the supply officer of the Brigade:

```
        Gallons gasoline                 30,000
        Gallons 600 W.                    1,000
        Gallons light gas cylinder oil    1,000
        Pounds hard grease                5,000
```

                                                S. D. Rockenbach,
                                                Brigadier General, U.S.A.

All units were in place by night of September 25-26.

OPERATIONS OF THE FIRST AMERICAN TANK BRIGADE

Plans for Tank Operations

The 14th and 17th Groups of French Tanks, the 344th Battalion less one company and the 345th Battalion less one company were assigned to operate in the sector of the 35th Division. Position of readiness: southwestern edge of COTES DE FORIMONT.[8] Position of departure, D minus 1 night: TRENCHES BOUREUILLES-VAUQUOIS.

---

[8] Editor's note: Also spelled "d'Forimont" in other sections of this report.

One company of the 344th Battalion and one company of the 345th Battalion were assigned to operate in the sector of the 28th Division. Position of readiness: ABANCOURT FARM. Point of departure: Small woods 4 kilometers north of ABANCOURT FARM.

The 344th Battalion supported the advance of the 28th and 35th Divisions. One company disposed west of the AIRE RIVER and two east. The 345th Battalion followed in support echelon at a distance of 1500 meters in rear of the front line, one company disposed west and two companies east of the river.

The 14th and 17th Groups (French) in reserve echelon were at a distance of 2,000 meters in the rear of the front line.

The original intention was to have the 344th Battalion support the advance to the American objective. At this point the 345th Battalion was to "leap-frog" and support the advance from that point on. The 14th and 17th Groups (French) were to go into action after passing the I Corps objective and support the advance as far as possible.

The repair and salvage company consisting of the 321st Company was established at CAMP FOURGOUS, 500 meters south of BRAINCOURT.

The repair and salvage company moved forward and established themselves at VARENNES, September 30th 1918.

Execution

September 26: Due to the serious resistance of the enemy, especially along the eastern edge of the FORET D'ARGONNE and in the vicinity of CHEPPY and VARENNES, and due also the lack of support of the Infantry, all the Tanks had contrary to plan entered the action before evening of the first day.

The 344th Battalion supporting the advance of the 28th and 35th Divisions left the positions of departure and advanced ahead of the Infantry at H-hour (5:30 a.m.)

On the morning of the 26th, Colonel G. S. Patton, Jr.,[9] commanding the brigade of Tanks, was wounded while getting Tanks forward and rallying disorganized Infantrymen to attack enemy resistance. Major Sereno E. Brett, commanding the 344th Battalion, was then placed in command of the brigade and continued so during the time covered by this report.[10]

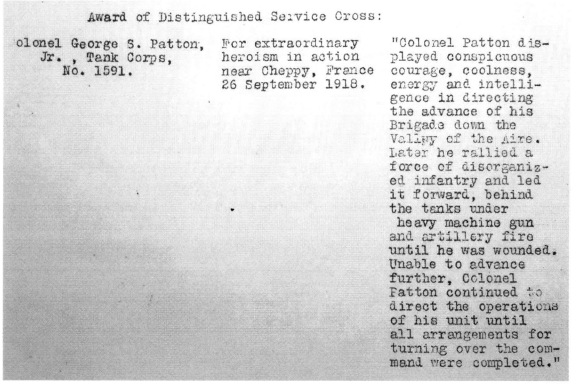

Image from archived Report.

The resistance encountered during the day was very severe, the chief resistance being machine gun fire, with, in addition, heavy artillery fire. The Tanks succeeded in reducing numerous machine gun nests that had proven troublesome and sometimes fatal to the Infantry advance. This resistance was

---

[9] Patton was a Lieutenant Colonel at the time of his injury but promoted to Colonel three weeks later (October 17). Martin Blumenson, The Patton Papers 1885-1940 (Boston: Houghton Mifflin Company, 1972), p. 624.

[10] However, Captain Ranulf Compton, Commander of the 345th Battalion, was placed in command of "all tanks on the front," including "the 14th and 17th French Tank Groups, Major Chanoine, Commanding, and the 344th and 345th Battalions, Tank Corps." George S. Patton, Jr., Ranulf Compton, War Diary 1918 (Silver Spring, MD: Dale Street Books, 2017), diary entry for September 27, 1918.

particularly strong east of VAUQUOIS HILL and in the town of VARENNES. The Tanks reached this latter named place at 9:30 a.m. The supporting Infantry reached VARENNES at 1:30 p.m. Those Tanks which were in operating condition continued the advance on the morning of the 27th, proceeding at times under the most adverse conditions of terrain and Infantry support. Forty-three Tanks were out of action on the morning of the 27th.

<u>September 27:</u> The Tanks on the left or west of the RIVER AIRE reorganized at BOUREUILLES on the night of September 26th. One the morning of the 27th they went forward with 11 Tanks. These advanced along the edge of the FORET D'ARGONNE northwest of VARENNES putting out machine guns and capturing a number of prisoners, all machine gunners. These were turned over to the Infantry.

On the right or east bank of the river there were repeated calls from the Infantry for help, but no concerted plan of attack seemed available. Two platoons of Tanks from Company "A" of the 344th Battalion went forward to support an attack of the plateau north of VERY.

<u>September 28:</u> Eighty-three Tanks were ready for action on the morning of the 28th. Requests had come in from the various Infantry divisions for help during the 27th. The 28th Division requested 10 Tanks, the 35th requested 40, and the 91st five Tanks for use as combat liaison between the 35th and 91st Divisions. To the 28th Division was assigned 15 Tanks, to the 35th was assigned 42 Tanks and to the 91st five Tanks with 27 Tanks in the brigade reserve. Of the 42 Tanks assigned to the 35th Division, six were French and 36 American.

On this date, Tanks took the town of APREMONT five times before the Infantry would enter, consolidate and exploit the success.

Throughout the day serious and well organized Tank defense was met, consisting of anti-Tank rifles, direct firing artillery, and frequent enemy standing barrages, which were brought down with little delay.

On this date the 14th and 17th Groups of French Tanks were withdrawn due to complete mechanical exhaustion by order of the Chief of Tank Corps.

September 29: Fifty-five Tanks were ready for action on the morning of the 29th. The repair and salvage worked all the night of the 28th to bring the number of Tanks to this total. The casualties were due to all causes, chiefly mechanical. During the day of the 29th, Captain Ranulf Compton, commanding the forward units, was ordered to furnish as many fresh crews as possible from his detachment and to withdraw as many crews from the front line as possible.

The Tanks on the left or west of the RIVER AIRE remained in APREMONT with the expectation of meeting a counterattack. The Tanks on the right bank of the AIRE, or eastern bank, moved to BAULNY acting as a reserve for the 35th Division. Late in the afternoon the Tanks were called upon to assist in meeting a counterattack directed from the MONTREBEAU WOODS and were ordered to hold the line BAULNY-ECLISFONTAINE.[11] This was done. Tank patrols were established to allow the Infantry to reorganize on the new line. The Tanks were withdrawn after dark.

September 30: On September 30th the Tanks were withdrawn to reserve positions in compliance with orders from the I Corps and then remained in reserve with a few exceptions until October 4th.

On the morning of September 30th, 20 Tanks were sent at the request of the 35th Division to assist in resisting a counterattack which was anticipated north of CHARPENTRY. Nothing developed, however, and the Tanks returned at 1:30 p.m. of the same day. Five Tanks were dispatched to SERIEUX FARM at the request of the same division. Nothing developed here and at 3:15 these Tanks also returned. Five Tanks patrolled northwest of APREMONT during the morning but no action developed.

The repair and salvage continued to repair the disabled Tanks and on the morning of October 1st, 61 Tanks were ready for action.

October 1: During the evening of September 30th, the 28th Division requested a group of eight Tanks to aid in a local attack west of APREMONT to the stream of CROISETTE. This attack was to start at 6:00 a.m. on October 1st. The enemy, however, attacked at 5:30. The Tanks were in place and

---

[11] Spelled "Eglisfontaine" in original.

rendered valuable assistance in dispersing and repulsing this attack. General Nolan, commanding the 28th Division, was on the ground and commended the Tank commanders for their valuable work.

The repairing and salvaging of the Tanks was considerably retarded because of the shelling in the forward areas where the Tanks were located. The repair parties suffered casualties.

October 4: On the 3rd of October, 89 Tanks were reported ready for action by the repair and salvage. (Situation as per report)

HEADQUARTERS - TANK CORPS - FIRST ARMY

3 Oct 18, 8:00 p.m.

From: Chief of Tank Corps, 1st Army

To: Asst. Chief of Staff, G-3, 1st Army
Subject: Status of Tank Troops

1. Attached to I Corps -

(a) 1st American Brigade has lost in fighting crews, killed and wounded: officers 53%, includes four out of six captains, 12 out of 24 lieutenants. Soldiers 25% - 65. Tanks ditched or disabled and under enemy's artillery fire - 70.
Ready to fight 72 Tanks with three crews. One days' normal fighting with an advance of 5 kilometers will enable me to maintain and fight 72 Tanks on the 5th and 6th, on the 7th I may be able to fight 48 Tanks, on the 8th 32, on the 9th 16 and on the 10th finished.
(b) Schneider Groupement mechanically broken down and returned to depot.

2. For the III Corps - two groups St. Chamond ready to fight on the 4th and 5th, one group to arrive ready to fight on the 6th and 7th. Then one group out of the first two ready to fight on the 7th and 8th then [sic] finished.

3. With the V Corps – 15th and 17th French Light Battalions ready to fight. 13th and 14th French Battalions ready to fight on the evening of the 6th. On the 8th and 9th probably able to fight one battalion, then they will have to withdraw for overhauling, rest and repair.

                                              S. D. Rockenbach,
                                      Brigadier General, U.S.A.

The dispositions for the attack on the 4th of October were as follows: Two companies of Tanks supported the advance of the 1st Division, which had replaced the 35th Division. One company supported the advance of the 28th Division. The Tanks went over at H-hour on the morning of October 4th.

The brigade reserve of 13 Tanks left VARENNES at 2:00 p.m. following the advance of the 1st Division. The support rendered to the Tanks by this division was excellent, and the division reported that the Tanks did effective work. These reciprocal reports no doubt resulted from the excellence of the liaison between the two units. The artillery fire encountered on this day was particularly accurate and severe. Strong resistance was encountered in the advance in the vicinity of HILL 240 in the sector of the 1st Division and along the FORET D'ARGONNE in the sector of the 28th Division. It was necessary for the brigade reserve to go into the action. Casualties in the personnel and material were particularly heavy.

October 5: Thirty Tanks were left in action on the morning of the 5th but failed to report due to excess mechanical trouble. This trouble was caused in a great many cases by the running of the Tanks a considerable distance from their positions of readiness to the positions of departure, varying usually between 10 and 20 kilometers. Fifteen of the 30 Tanks were sent to the 1st Division and the remaining to the 28th. Owing to the continued advance of the Tanks the machinery was in very poor condition and a great many minor difficulties from time to time retarded the advance.

October 6: On the morning of the 6th, 17 Tanks were left ready for action but under directions from the I Corps, all Tanks were drawn back to the reserve positions. The Tanks did no fighting on this date but 24 were made ready for the 7th.

October 7: One company was ordered to support an attack made by the 28th Division, and as only eight Tanks were available on the west side of the RIVER AIRE they were dispatched. One of these struck a mine and was disabled but the rest reported.

October 8: Twenty-six Tanks were ready for action on the morning of the 8th. Five of these were in good mechanical condition and the remaining 21 might have been expected to stand one day's fighting. However, they were not used as the 28th and 82nd Divisions to whom they had been detailed could not use them because of the unsuitability of the terrain.

October 9: Thirty-five Tanks were in condition on the morning of the 9th and were placed at the disposal of the 82nd Division, which had replaced the 28th [Division]. But they were not called for.

October 11: Forty-eight Tanks were on the morning of the 11th, reported to be in condition. At midnight of the 10th, 23 Tanks left the town of VARENNES to report to Commanding General, 164th Brigade of the 82nd Division. The request had been for five Tanks but due to the poor condition of the engines only three of these Tanks reached their destination at FLIREY, the others falling out along the way. The three Tanks were rejected by the Commanding General and they returned to their posts.

The Tanks took part in no further activity, but were all withdrawn to VARENNES for extensive overhauling to put them back into battle condition.

October 13 – 16: On this date the 1st Provisional Company of the 304th Brigade was formed with the following organization:
Captain Courtney Barnard, Commanding,
10 officers,
140 enlisted men.

A reserve crew was provided for every Tank. On the 14th of October the Provisional Company was equipped at VARENNES. On the afternoon of the 14th, this company left for EXERMONT to establish its post of command there.

On the 15th the commanding officer of the Provisional Company was directed to prepare for an attack on the morning of the 16th.

On the 14th the brigade received a letter of commendation from the Commanding General, 1st Division for the energy and efficiency of the members.

On the 15th the 304th Brigade less the Provisional Company returned to the 302nd Tank Center.

On October 16, the Tanks supported the 42nd Division on this day southwest of ST. GEORGES. Ten Tanks entered the fight and reached their objectives. The Infantry did not follow and the Tanks returned. Large bodies of the enemy were dispersed during this advance.

Subsequent Operations. From October 16 to November 1, the Provisional Company remained in reserve at EXERMONT. On November 1, 15 Tanks took part in the general advance, five being directed against ST. GEORGES and 10 against LANDRES-ET-ST. GEORGES and vicinity.

The work of these Tanks was commended by the Commanding General, 2nd Division, with whom they were operating. Three of these Tanks penetrated as far as the Corps Objective and one entered the southern outskirts of BUZANCY. North of LANDRES-ET-ST. GEORGES three Tanks flanked and captured a battery of 77's complete.

On November 2nd the Provisional Company assembled at BAYONVILLE and remained there until their equipment was taken over by the 306th Brigade. This Brigade had been organized at the Center, brought up, had repaired and stood ready to carry on the fight with 96 Tanks when the armistice was announced.

Liaison. The 304th Brigade used the Infantry axis of liaison. Liaison officers were at division and corps message center; French speaking officers with the French Groups of Tanks.

Liaison with all units was effected by motorcycle, telephone, runner, pigeons, and by visual signals. Aeroplanes rendered valuable assistance.

Medical Detachment. The medical detachment worked with the utmost vigor establishing forward dressing stations, many times under shell fire. A large percentage of evacuations were handled by the brigade medical detachment. It is to be noted, however, that the medical detachment was far too small to properly take care of all units of the command. There was a noticeable absence of stretcher bearers who had they been present would not only have saved lives but would have prevented fighting men carrying wounded to the rear.

Supplies. The supply of gasoline and equipment to the Tanks and of rations to the troops was excellent, the chief difficulty arising out of the congestion of the traffic and the bad condition of the roads.

The main supply dump was at VARENNES. Supplies were carried to the forward dumps and units by motor trucks. These motor trucks used the roads as indicated on the corps circulation map.

Artillery Preparation. Smoke shells were used in the rolling barrage and placed along the edges of the woods and near command posts.

The rolling barrage moving along at a steady rate of speed got beyond the Infantry and Tanks, who were unable to follow it due to the resistance. This fact allowed the enemy to reorganize and to offer a tenacious resistance.

The intelligence work in discovering anti-Tank guns was deficient. Enemy batteries designated as Tank defense were not only in large numbers but were not disorganized or registered upon, in our artillery preparation.

Casualties-Material. Of 92 Tanks accounted for on October 16, 1918, 17 were struck by shells, six of them being demolished. Four were pierced by anti-Tank rifles. The only Tanks whose turrets were pierced by anti-Tank rifles were Tanks with round cast turrets.

Out of a total of 141 Tanks engaged, 140 have been accounted for. One Tank may have been captured by the enemy. (Since located and brought in.)

Tactical Conclusions

1. Field officers in their demands on the Tanks did not seem to realize their limitations and especially the fact that Tanks must have Infantry operating with them, if they are to be successfully employed.

2. Lack of liaison between Tanks and Infantry not only made it difficult to keep track of the operations of the Tanks but also hampered the efficiency of the Tank operations.

3. Infantry should act as though Tanks were not present and not expect Tanks to overcome resistance and wait expecting Tanks to attempt to consolidate a success.

4. Tanks should not be used for reconnaissance purposes.

5. Reduce to a minimum the distance between the position of readiness and the position of departure. The report bears out the fact that Tanks cannot sustain a prolonged march without being overhauled and put in order.

6. The first essential of a successful Tank operation is a complete preliminary reconnaissance of the terrain over which the Tanks are to operate. Hence the reconnaissance staff must be well organized with perfect liaison between company, battalion, and brigade reconnaissance officers. Orders from higher commanders effecting an operation must arrive in time to allow the Tank commander at least four hours of daylight to make and foresee in time the reconnaissance to be made for the proper disposition of Tank units and present in time the plan for the operation to the individual Tank commanders.

7. The enemy artillery is the dangerous adversary of the Tanks. The conditions indispensable to the success of an operation undertaken with Tanks are in consequence, a particularly careful neutralization of the enemy artillery; special disposition to work against enemy defense batteries close to the line; the blinding of observations posts which look upon the terrain of the attack, and augmentation of the capacity of shell explosions by the employment of smoke shells.

8. The tenacity and skill with which the enemy employed his defense weapons in the ARGONNE enabled the Tanks to demonstrate their value as a weapon of attack. The miserably few available and their work leaves no doubt as to what would have been their value, had we had them in large numbers as was planned.

OPERATIONS OF THE FRENCH TANKS

Plans for Tank Operations

<u>ZONE of V Corps.</u> The light battalions were attached as follows:

13th Battalion with the 37th Division
14th Battalion with the 79th Division
15th Battalion with the 79th Division
17th Battalion in reserve for the Corps
Groupement XI with the 79th Division

It was arranged for the 15th Battalion to operate with the 4th Division - right division of the III Corps.

On D-1 the Tank units were at their point of departure, northern point of GESNES WOODS. They were to reach this point at H plus 8. If the attack developed satisfactorily they were to be at the following points at H plus 12:

13th Battalion east of GESNES
14th Battalion CUNEL WOODS
15th Battalion BEUGE WOODS
Groupement XI, CUNEL WOODS

If unsatisfactorily, the Tanks were to take orders—after H plus 8—from the divisions to which they were attached. Preparations necessary to permit Tanks to cross:-

1. The 1st American position.
2. The German systems in MONTFAUCON WOODS.

A path was to be made by the 37th and 79th Divisions as far as the northern border of MONTFAUCON WOODS.

For this purpose each division was to assign one company Pioneers to the Tanks.

The work to be performed by the 79th Division was to be directed by Commandant Herlaut commanding Groupement XI; that to be done by the 37th, to be directed by Commandant Duclos commanding the 13th Battalion.

Liaison: the commanders of the light battalions to accompany the generals commanding the divisions. Company commanders with the brigade or regimental commanders.

Protective measures taken by Tanks: batteries were assigned to counter-battery fire on anti-Tank guns. The barrage to include a certain amount of smoke shells.

ZONE of I Corps. During the night of D-1 Groupement IV to proceed to point of departure, west corner of COTES DE FORIMONT near the NEUVILLY-VARENNES ROAD.

At 0 hour the groups to leave the point of departure in column and in the following order: AS 17, AS 14 - to follow a course laid out in the itinerary, ravine west of BUZEMONT, western corner of ROSSIGNOL COMMUNICATION TRENCH, CHEPPY, VERY.

In reality the groups were not to participate until reaching the Corps objective—VERY—a point to be attained at H plus 4:30. Nonetheless the captain commanding A.S. 17 was to accompany the colonel commanding the leading Infantry regiment, in order to call in his group if the Infantry were attacked.

Rallying point, west of VERY.

Preparations: A platoon and a half of American Pioneers was placed at the disposal of Groupement IV to complete the contemplated path, this to be staff of the groupement. On reaching VERY the American Pioneers and accompanying Infantry were to be divided among the two groups.

Liaison: The commander of the group to establish his command post at the following successive points:

The Brigade over the BRANIERE RIVER.
The BITLIS SYSTEM.
The outlet north of CHEPPY.
The VERY MILL.

Protective Measures: One battery of the 209th Light Artillery selected for counter-battery fire on anti-Tank pieces.

Execution

From Colonel Wahl's (French) report:[12]

Operations on September 26

ZONE of V Corps. The Tanks left their points of departure at 0 hour, but the work on the paths through the German Lines progressed slowly. The terrain was soggy and unfavorable, and instead of a company of Pioneers each division sent but 100 men. At 1:00 p.m. the 13th Battalion leading was on a terrain a trifle more favorable, 400 meters south of CUISY WOODS. At this moment, the Infantry (79th Division) was stopped 200 meters south of CUISY WOODS by intense machine gun fire.

The captains commanding the 337th and 339th Companies were asked to intervene by the Infantry though this Infantry did not belong to the division to which the Tanks were attached—the 37th. Two sections were engaged, and at 5:00 p.m. CUISY WOODS was cleared and the woods were occupied by the Infantry.

At 7:00 p.m. the 339th Company engaged one section in the direction of MONTFAUCON and let the Infantry to the defenses south of there.

In leaving the path to aid the Infantry the 13th Light Battalion left a number of Tanks behind. The splitting up of sections and the accompaniment of strange Infantry over a terrain that had never been reconnoitered was patently contrary to regulations, but the Tanks nonetheless rendered great service. The Infantry, inexperienced, and with little leadership, remained stationary: it was imperative that the Tanks should precede them in order to lead them forward.

Meanwhile the 14th, 15th and 17th Light Battalions which had been delayed in MONTFAUCON WOODS awaiting the completion of the paths began to arrive at the assembly point (northern border of CUISY WOODS) at 5:30 p.m.

Groupement XI did not reach the northern edge of MONTFAUCON WOODS until the morning of the 27th.

---

[12] Portions edited out, as indicated by five stars (* * * * *). See "1st French Brigade at Meuse-Argonne," in the supporting documents for full report.

During the night of the 26th-27th the four battalions (light) assembled in CUISY WOODS.

Throughout the day, the protective measures (artillery) were not able to function.

The congestion of the one-way road prevented the bringing up of smoke shells, and the batteries were not able to follow by reason of the soggy conditions and the blocking.

* * * * *

Operations on September 27

The 13th Battalion was at the disposition of the 73rd Brigade (37th Division). The General in command of this brigade asked at 2:30 p.m. for one section to attack in the direction of CIERGES. This section took up its position of departure but the order was countermanded. At 8:00 p.m. the section returned to the rallying point.

The commander of the 14th Battalion had the greatest difficulty in rejoining the commander of the brigade to which he was attached.

Meanwhile the commander of the 342nd Company, who had maintained liaison with the commander of the 313th Regiment Infantry launched in concert with the latter a rapid attack with a view to encircling MONTFAUCON.

MONTFAUCON was encircled. The Infantry did not follow, but succeeded nonetheless in infiltrating into the village.

The 15th Light Battalion assigned the 343rd Company to the 314th Regiment.

The 15th Light Battalion assigned the 344th Company to the 315th Regiment.

At 5:30 p.m. the sections preceding the Infantry cleaned up the terrain between MONTFAUCON and SEPTSARGES, the southern edge of BEUGE WOODS, and the ridge north of NANTILLOIS.

The Infantry followed very slowly and though NANTILLOIS was evacuated remained 1500 meters south.

The companies rallied at nightfall south of FAYEL WOODS.

* * * * *

Operations on September 28

The general commanding the division asked the commander of the 13th Battalion for three sections with which to support an attack by the 74th Brigade upon CIERGES.

Two sections were immediately sent to their positions of departure, (85.73), but the attack was put off till the morrow, the Infantry not being ready. The sections remained at their position of departure.

The commanders of the 340th and 341st Companies (14th Battalion) succeeded in finding the colonel of the 316th Regiment, and offered him their services. The objective was very ill-defined—advance toward the north; first attack BEUGE WOODS.

But there were no Germans in BEUGE WOODS. There were some Americans south of WOOD 286. The Tanks cleared the edges west of WOOD 268 and 250 and reached MADELEINE WOODS, but though they returned several times to lead the Infantry forward, the latter recoiled before the artillery fire.

The 79th Division which had that morning taken BEUGE WOODS and the ridge north of NANTILLOIS received orders to continue the attack toward CUNEL and to reduce the woods on each side of the NANTILLOIS-CUNEL ROAD.

The 344th Company supported the advance of the 158th Brigade. They destroyed machine guns, and led the Infantry to the attack on the wood south of CUNEL.

But the Tanks encountered heavy artillery fire. The Infantry stopped. The Tanks got orders to retire. Two received direct hits. The Infantry immediately left the conquered terrain.

Groupement XI comprising but four batteries of three Tanks each, attacked simultaneously with two batteries to the east of the road, and two to the west.

The Tanks destroyed numerous machine guns. Some reached PUNAIS[13] FARM and MADELEINE FARM, but the Infantry did not pass WOOD 268. The Tanks withdrew to TUILERIE WOODS, and on the 29th to the north of MONTFAUCON WOODS.

---

[13] Spelled "Punals" in supporting documents, "1st French Brigade at Meuse-Argonne."

Operations on September 29 – October 3

The three sections of the 13th Battalion awaiting at their positions of departure since the day before were placed at the disposal of the 148th Regiment Infantry to attack CIERGES. The sections went into action between ANDON and EMONT WOODS. No resistance developed at first, but from CIERGES on the heavy machine gun fire stopped the Infantry. One section advanced toward the village. The Infantry retreated, abandoning the Tanks. The two remaining sections withdrew, but the section which had proceeded toward CUNEL did not return.

The 14th Battalion took position for an attack which was countermanded September 30th.

The 15th Battalion placed the 344th Company at the disposal of the 138th Brigade to re-undertake its attack of the day before. The Tanks reduced MADELEINE FARM and OGNON WOODS. The Infantry followed only as far as OGNON WOODS. The Tanks were withdrawn at 6:00 p.m. Five Tanks were broken down in our lines, one of them struck by a shell. During the night the Infantry withdrew 1,500 meters, in the face of light bombardment, leaving five Tanks (the broken down ones), and two which had remained on the terrain from the day before in the enemy's hands. (See letter from Commanding General 37th Division to Commanding General French Tanks, 30 Sept 1918.)[14]

The Americans carried out the reliefs of the various divisions, and their establishment in positions.

Unfortunately orders and counter-orders necessitated the units changing positions for attacks which were revoked every day. The 14th Battalion suffered especially from these movements.

October 3, the 13th and 14th Battalions were withdrawn to HESSE FOREST.

General Conditions of the Operations.
Methods of Using Tanks from October 4 – 10

After a period of reorganization and reliefs, the V Corps was to affect a joint attack with the III Corps.

---

[14] Not archived with Report in Carlisle.

The 32nd Division replaced the 37th.
The 3rd replaced the 79th.
The boundaries of the V and III Corps were slightly modified.

October 2, Groupement XI was placed at the disposal of the III Corps, specifically with the 4th Division Infantry, the left division.

But on October 3 on reaching the command post of the 4th Division Commander Herlaut learned that the sector of the 4th Division had been taken over during the night of October 3-4 by the 80th Division, and vice versa. This relief hindered a great deal the establishment of liaisons which had been completely affected with the 4th Division.

ZONE of III Corps. The 80th Division to attack in depth, the regiments in line in the brigades; in each regiment the battalions in depth.

The groupement was reorganized into a scratch group of 5 x 4 batteries, three of them containing four Tanks each, and one of them containing three.

One battery was attached to the assaulting battalion on the right; the other two (of four Tanks each) were assigned to the assaulting battalion of the left. The three-Tank battery was to support the supporting battalion—as a cleaning up battery.

Objective: PULTIER WOODS - north of CUNEL.

* * * * *

ZONE of V Corps. The 15th Light Battalion was attached to the 3rd Division. The 17th Light Battalion was attached to the 32nd Division.

The disposition of troops in the 3rd Division, to be the same as in the 80th.

The 343rd Company (two sections) attached to the battalion assaulting on the right. The 344th (three sections) to that on the left. The 345th Company (one section) to the supporting battalion on the left.

Objective: ROMAGNE-CUNEL.

The evening of October 2, the 32nd Division changed its order of attack. It was decided to attack with brigades in line instead of in depth.

The 17th Light Battalion gave one company to each brigade. The 3rd Company was held in reserve.

Objectives: the heights north of GESNES.

D-Day fixed for October 4; 0 hour for 5:25 a.m.

Operations on October 4

ZONE of III Corps. The Group XI attacked with three batteries of three Tanks each, the fourth battery having been broken up to complete the attacking batteries.

At first the attack proceeded normally, with the Tanks leading; then it stopped south of OGNON WOODS. The Tanks cleared the borders of OGNON WOODS along the southern edge, called the Infantry and returned several times to find them. About 11:00 a.m. the Tanks were caught in a heavy artillery fire, and being unable to persuade the Infantry to leave the WILPRE SPRINGS RAVINE, withdrew.

ZONE of V Corps. The Tanks cleared the banks east of ANDON, the western borders of CUNEL WOODS, and attacked CUNEL and ROMAGNE. The Infantry followed well, took MAMELLE TRENCH, and organized on the EAST-WEST ROAD, about 300 meters to the north. Owing to severe losses they remained on this line.

Many Tanks were held fast in the swampy banks of the rivulets that cut the terrain.

During the night the Infantry abandoned a part of its gains.

The 15th Light Battalion was withdrawn and rejoined the other Tanks October 6, at CAMP CLAIRS CHENES.

As the 32nd Division had not attacked at 0 hour owing to being unprepared, the Tanks went to the rear.

At 4:00 p.m. the attack was resumed; the Tanks advanced as far as GESNES, but the Infantry did not follow.

Operations on October 5

ZONE of III Corps. At 11:30 p.m. October 4, the III Corps decided to resume the attack on the north of WILPERS SPRINGS. A scratch battery of four Tanks was organized. It was agreed with the colonel commanding the 318th Infantry that the Tanks were to lead at 100 meters and would return to fetch the Infantry if it did not follow.

The attack was launched at 10:20 a.m. At 1:35 the Infantry had ceased following the Tanks. The only Tank in running order retired. At 3:00 p.m. October 5, the general commanding the III Corps released Groupement XI. The six and seven remaining Tanks retired to SIVRY WOODS.

ZONE of V Corps. The 32nd Division decided to resume the attack that had broken down the day before. Two sections of the 17th Battalion were engaged. The Tanks cleared GESNES, the woods to the east, HILL 235, and MARINE and CHENE-SEC WOODS.

Operations on October 9

ZONE of V Corps. The 17th Light Battalion received order to assemble at CAMP POMMIERS near RECICOURT with a view to being subsequently employed. Nevertheless, the 351st Company was left at the disposal of the 32nd Division to take part in the attack that had been prepared the 7th and 8th by reconnaissance.

Objectives: ROMAGNE and the heights of the west.

The 32nd Division had one brigade in line; the regiments arranged side by side; each regiment had two battalions in the first line.

One section was assigned to each of the attacking battalions. One section in reserve.

Axis of Attack: CIERGES-ROMAGNE ROAD.

One section to the east; one to the west.

0 hour fixed for 8:30 a.m. but at the order of the general commanding the 63rd Brigade the Tanks left alone at 11:00 p.m. They passed the Infantry at MAMELLE TRENCH, and one supported the attack on ROMAGNE which was taken.

At 4:00 p.m. the 341st was released.

October 10 the 17th Light Battalion was assembled at POMMIERS CAMP.

* * * * *

Tactical Conclusions

On the greater part of the attacking front the Tanks supported an Infantry which not only knew nothing of fighting with Tanks but what is more had never been under fire and were not skilled in Infantry combat.

Groupement IV supported by the 35th Division, which had seen some experience, obtained good results. October 4, the 14th Battalion attacked with the 3rd Division, which had already seen action; here again the ground won by the Tanks was occupied.

September 26 the attack enjoyed a partial success. The forward movement being stopped the effort immediately dwindled. No orders were forthcoming, and the Tanks in order to keep busy were reduced to participating in minor operations until September 29. Even these minor operations were often suggested by the commanders of the battalions or the companies. Sometimes the Tanks would lead the Infantry forward.

The 4th, 5th, and 9th of October the American command succeeded in giving impetus to the whole. The results were much better, and the gains realized were partially taken advantage of by the Infantry's occupation.

General Conclusions[15]

1. We were unable to remedy the defect reported on by Major Parker in May 1917. Tank units were never able to get that acquaintance and training with the Infantry which is essential to their successful employment, but under the circumstances at the time, and the results obtained, could it have been done better? We think not.

2. Tank tactics must be very elastic. We teach for normal operation. There never has been anything according to the rules and principles of the art of war, as written, in the operations of the U.S. Army. War is abnormal. Tanks are to assist the Infantry. If the Infantry need no assistance, do not employ Tanks. If there is wire to cut, send Tanks that reach it ahead. When machine guns have been located, send Tanks after them. The U.S. Army will always have to employ green troops. With green troops Tank tactics should control. Tell a truck driver to take

---

[15] Rockenbach narrative resumes.

his truck to APREMONT, he will do it. One did it at a time when reports show that no life could exist on the road from CHEPPY to APREMONT. Men ordered to follow certain Tanks at a distance of 100 yards did it; reports show they went through hellfire in doing it. Detachments of Pioneers ordered to follow Tanks and make a road for them did it. Hence, it is thought that with green troops, a battalion of Infantry should be ordered to follow a company of Tanks, given a task all can understand. Given seasoned divisions trained with and assisted by Tanks nothing can stop them.

    3. Moral Effect. The evening of the 29th of September was, as may be recalled, a bit gloomy. My anxiety had taken me through VARENNES, CHEPPY, CHARPENTRY, BAULNY, VERY and MONTFAUCON. Report was called for as to what the Tanks could do. Reply was made: Put the 1st Division with the remaining Tanks and we can go through hell (Sedan). The Boche never got over his fear of Tanks, they filled him with terror. Of course, now that it is over, to the survivors it was like the bear story. The Tank said "Boch!" and the Boche said "Boch." The Tank rattled its tread, the Boche unable to make such a noise as that, he ere [sic] – he beat it. It is hoped the operations of the Tanks with the First American Army will cause serious study of them.

AMERICAN TANKS WITH THE BRITISH E.F.

The 301st Battalion having completed its training at the British Tank Center at Wool, and our heavy Tanks not being ready, the British proposal to equip the battalion with their Mark V and operate it with their forces in France was accepted.

Their operations were as follows:

301ST BATTALION

The 301st American Tank Battalion arrived at the British Tank Corps Training Center, England, on April 10, 1918, direct from America.

The battalion was preceded by a number of American officers and noncommissioned officers from France, who were trained as instructors.

On August 23, the battalion, consisting of 68 officers and 777 enlisted men, under the command of Major R. B. Harrison, embarked at Southampton and disembarked at HAVRE on August 24 whence they proceeded to BERMICOURT CAMP, Tank Corps Area, in France.

Parties of the battalion were attached to various British Tank brigades for short periods, so that they might learn as much as possible of the British Tank tactics in France.

On September 2 the battalion relieved the 10th British Tank Battalion in the BIENVILLERS and ACHIET-LE-GRAND area, and came under the command of the 1st British Tank Brigade. At this date the battalion was in possession of 47 Mark V Tanks.

On September 18, the battalion was transferred to the 4th British Tank Brigade, and on 22nd moved with all its Tanks to EQUANCOURT (Val. A.G.)

The battalion was assigned to the 27th American Division, less seven Tanks which were placed in the American Corps reserve for the attack on September 29.

Thirty-four Tanks of the 301st Battalion started at Zero,[16] but owing to the very heavy and accurate hostile artillery fire, very heavy casualties were

---

[16] O hour.

received, although a certain number of hostile machine gun nests were knocked out. The casualties amounted to 112 all ranks.

On October 6, [a] composite company was formed which [was] assigned to the 118th Infantry Brigade, 30th American Division, for an attack on the APREMONT-BRANCOURT Line on October 8.

Nineteen Tanks started and affected a complete success. All objectives were taken and very great assistance was rendered to the Infantry. Very many casualties were caused to the German machine gunners. This action was very successful in all respects and gave great confidence to the battalions.

Twenty-five Tanks of the battalion were again attached to the II Corps (American), who had for their objective the line west of BUSIGNY, eastern edge of SABLIERE WOODS – west of BOHAIN (ST QUENTIN F.1).

The difficulty of the operations was the uncertainty whether the RIVER SELLE would prove a Tank obstacle or not; a reconnaissance two days previous to the attack showed that Tanks could cross the river at certain points.

Of the 25 Tanks which started, 19 crossed the river and rendered assistance to the Infantry, but were hampered in their movements by the density of the fog, which caused the Tanks to lose their direction.

The 301st Battalion was transferred from the 4th British Tank Brigade to the 2nd British Tank Brigade on October 19.

The nine Tanks of the battalion were allotted to the 1st and 6th British Divisions for the attack on the high ground overlooking the CANAL DE LA SAMBRE A L'OISE[17] between CATILLON and BOIS L'EVEQUE, and the villages of FONTAINE-AU-BOIS, ROBARSART, and BOUSIES.

All Tanks started on October 23 and greatly assisted the Infantry. No Tank was put out of action.

The battalion was placed in Fourth Army Reserve on October 24 and on the next day in general headquarters reserve.

Major R. I. Sasse took over the command of the battalion on October 29.

Nine Tanks of the 301st Battalion were assembled at MONTAY ready for an attack on November 4, but were not used, and subsequently were transferred to Third Army Reserve.

---

[17] Sambre-Oise Canal.

The Battalion was transferred to the 5th British Tank Brigade on November 19 and on that date entrained at LE QUESNOY for MACIC-COURT [sic].

On November 23, General Rockenbach, commanding the American Tank Corps, inspected the battalion and expressed himself highly pleased on the way the 301st Battalion had acquitted itself during its short stay in France.

The Battalion moved to SAULTY on December 11 where it is now located and is engaged on Winter Training.

306TH REPAIR AND SALVAGE COMPANY

The 306th American Repair and Salvage Company was formed in America on July 24, 1918, under the command of Captain Bull.

This company embarked from America on August 14, disembarked at Liverpool, and proceeded to the British Tank Corps Training Center, Bovington Camp, Wool.

On arrival at the Wool Training Center, the company was placed under the command of Central Workshops (Training Center). It also rendered great assistance in repairing Tanks which had broken down on the Tracks.

On October 15, this company embarked for France. It arrived at Blingle Camp, Tank Corps Area, on October 21 where it was placed under the orders of the British Tank Corps Central Workshops, and assisted to repair Tanks.

On November 30, the company proceeded to the BAPAUME area to salve and repair damaged Tanks. During a period of five weeks this company has salved and repaired over 20 Tanks.

SUPPORTING DOCUMENTS

Major Sereno E. Brett. Source: https://commons.wikimedia.org/wiki/File:Sereno_E._Brett.jpg. Brett assumed command of the Tank Brigade after Patton was wounded.

Lieutenant Colonel Patton at center with Major Sereno E. Brett on his left as they prepare to review Brett's Tank Battalion. Source: <u>Armor</u>, July-August 1988, p. 34.

ORGANIZATION TANK CORPS 1ST ARMY

September 10, 1918

HEADQUARTERS

CHIEF OF TANK CORPS (Commanding) - Brigadier General S. D. Rockenbach, USA
Personal Staff – Second Lieutenant Frederick B. Bond, T.C. AIDE-DE-CAMP

STAFF

CHIEF OF STAFF	Lieutenant Colonel D. D. Pullen, Tank Corps (CE)
ASST. CHIEF OF STAFF	Major Joseph Viner, Tank Corps (Cav)
ADJUTANT	First Lieutenant William Miller, Tank Corps
Enlisted Strength	2
Attached	<u>4</u>
Total	6

1st BRIGADE (American)

COMMANDER	Lieutenant Colonel George S. Patton, Jr., Tank Corps

STAFF

ADJUTANT	Captain Edmund N. Hebert, Tank Corps
SUPPLY OFFICER	Captain W. S. Etheridge, Tank Corps
RECONNAISSANCE OFFICER	First Lieutenant Maurice H. Knowles, Tank Corps
TACTICAL OFFICER	First Lieutenant Harry E. Gibbs, Tank Corps
SIGNAL OFFICER	First Lieutenant Paul S. Edwards, S.C.
Enlisted Strength	7

TROOPS

326th BATTALION, TANK CORPS (American)[18]

COMMANDER	Major Sereno E. Brett, Tank Corps (Infantry)

STAFF

ADJUTANT	First Lieutenant Theo. J. Sledge, Tank Corps
SUPPLY OFFICER	First Lieutenant Roswell King, Tank Corps
REPAIR UNIT	First Lieutenant Fred C. Winters, Tank Corps
RECONNAISSANCE	

---

[18] 326th redesignated the 344th and 327th redesignated the 345th in September 1918. <u>Order of Battle of the United States Land Forces in the World War (1917-19)</u>, Part 2 (Washington, D.C.: United States Government Printing Office, 1949), p. 1545.

OFFICER	Second Lieutenant George B. Heilner, Tank Corps
GAS OFFICER	First Lieutenant Harry G. Borland, Tank Corps
SURGEON	First Lieutenant Lewis H. Howard, M.D.
	Enlisted Strength 63
COMPANY "A"	Captain Harry Hodges Semmes
	First Lieutenant Leslie H. Buckley
	Second Lieutenant Julian K. Morrison
	Second Lieutenant Earl Shirk
	Second Lieutenant Walter Rattray
	Second Lieutenant Edward McCluer (Attached)
	Second Lieutenant Gordon M. Grant (Attached)
	Enlisted Strength 89
COMPANY "B"	Captain Newell P. Weed
	First Lieutenant John Castles
	Second Lieutenant Daniel Helmich
	Second Lieutenant Stephen L. Conrey
	Second Lieutenant Edward Bowes (Attached)
	Second Lieutenant E. E. Wood
	Enlisted Strength 90
COMPANY "C"	Captain Math L. English
	First Lieutenant Loyall F. Sewall
	Second Lieutenant John Dunn
	Second Lieutenant Roscoe J. Perry (Attached)
	Second Lieutenant George Booth
	Second Lieutenant H. A. Wood
	Enlisted Strength 92

327th BATTALION, TANK CORPS (American)

COMMANDER	Captain Ranulf Compton, Tank Corps
	STAFF
ADJUTANT	First Lieutenant Lawrence C. Vidal, Tank Corps
SUPPLY OFFICER	First Lieutenant Gus Struyk, Tank Corps
REPAIR UNIT	First Lieutenant Tom W. Saul, Tank Corps
GAS OFFICER	Second Lieutenant Clarence W. Cleworth, Tank Corps
RECONNAISSANCE OFFICER	First Lieutenant Harry W. Bolan, Tank Corps
SURGEON	First Lieutenant Alphonse Isom, M.C.
	First Lieutenant Ernest A. Higgins (Attached)

	Second Lieutenant Lester L. Levin (Attached)
	Enlisted Strength 36
COMPANY "A"	Captain Dean M. Gilfillan
	First Lieutenant Thomas G. Brown
	Second Lieutenant Raymond F. Erhard
	Second Lieutenant Thomas D. Steel
	Second Lieutenant Harry M. Mayne
	Second Lieutenant John W. Roy (Attached)
	Enlisted Strength 93
COMPANY "B"	Captain William H. Williams
	First Lieutenant John W. Fordyce
	Second Lieutenant Joe S. Gamble
	Second Lieutenant Darwin T. Phillips
	Second Lieutenant Edward J. Mitchell
	Second Lieutenant Harry D. Heitz (Attached)
COMPANY "C"	Captain Courtney H. Barnard
	First Lieutenant Horace C. Nelms
	Second Lieutenant Joseph R. Younglove
	Second Lieutenant J. W. Gleason (Attached)
	Second Lieutenant Guy Chamberlain (Attached)
	Second Lieutenant John F. Carson (Attached)

316th COMPANY (R & S – American)

COMMANDER	Captain Ellis Baldwin, Tank Corps
	First Lieutenant Jesse L. Thompson, T.C.
	Second Lieutenant Aloysius J. Kelley, T.C.
	Second Lieutenant Don C. Wilson, T.C.
	Enlisted Strength 60

- ATTACHED –

IV Groupement French (See French Troops)

3rd BRIGADE (American)
(Headquarters only for liaison with French Troops)

COMMANDER	Lieutenant Colonel D. D. Pullen, Tank Corps (CE)
	(Chief of Staff, T.C. 1st Army)
	STAFF (Attached)

ASS'T TO COL PULLEN	Lieutenant Colonel R. F. Fowler, C of E
ADJUTANT	First Lieutenant H. J. Ellis, Tank Corps
SUPPLY OFFICER	Captain S. S. Garrett, Tank Corps
LIAISON OFFICERS	First Lieutenant Duboin, French Army
	Second Lieutenant F. T. Murphy, Tank Corps
RECONNAISSANCE OFFICERS	H. G. Halleck, Tank Corps
	First Lieutenant C. G. Burgess, Cavalry
	First Lieutenant W. A. Choquette, Tank Corps
	First Lieutenant H. L. Harris, Tank Corps
	First Lieutenant H. G. Hawes, Tank Corps
	First Lieutenant H. C. Pennoyer, Tank Corps
	First Lieutenant H. C. Jennings, Tank Corps
	First Lieutenant C. J. Sonstelie, Tank Corps
	Second Lieutenant C. T. Barnard, Tank Corps
	Second Lieutenant G. R. Chamberlain, Cavalry
	Second Lieutenant C. R. May, Tank Corps
	Enlisted Strength 57
	Interpreter Attached (French) 1
	58

FRENCH HEADQUARTERS

COMMANDER	Lieutenant Colonel Emile Wahl, Artillery

STAFF

CHIEF OF STAFF	Captain Jean Pierre, Infty
ASST. CHIEF OF STAFF	Second Lieutenant Lucian Chelli, Artillery
TECHNICAL	First Lieutenant Alban de Virel, Tank Corps

505th REGIMENT

COMMANDANT	Chef de Battalion MARE
OFFICERS ADJOINTS	Captain d'Armancourt
	Lieutenant Moreton[19]
	Sous-Lieutenant Pernot[20]

---

[19] Equivalent to U.S. Army First Lieutenant.
[20] Second Lieutenant. Abbreviated S/Lieutenant.

XIII B.C.L.

COMMANDANT	Chef de Battalion DUCLOS L.A.
OFFICERS ADJOINTS	Lieutenant Cossett E. R.
	Sous-Lieutenant Gistucci, X.J.J.
	Sous-Lieutenant Recamier L.P.G.
	Med. Auxil. Jondeau L.E.M.
A.S. 337	Captaine Liaras G.J.O.G.
A.S. 338	Lieutenant Laticule Y.M.
A.S. 339	Lieutenant Hamel H.M.

XIV B.C.L.

COMMANDANT	Chef de Battalion GUILLOT J.G.
OFFICERS ADJOINTS	Lieutenant Paul A.J.C.
	Sous-Lieutenant Bellanger E.F.
	Aspirant Bloch, H.M.
	Medec. A-M. Vegeas
A.S. 340	Captaine Maitre, J.L.R.
A.S. 341	Captaine Toutain J.F.
A.S. 342	Lieutenant Jacquot A.M.

XV B.C.L.

COMMANDANT	Chef de Battalion RICHARD E.L.
OFFICERS ADJOINTS	Lieutenant Haller A.A.J.
	Lieutenant St. Frison L.H.
	Sous-Lieutenant Ratheaux H.P.L.
	Med. A-M Andoli
A.S. 343	Captain Brunet de Monthelie A.A.
A.S. 344	Lieutenant More-Chevalier P.
A.S. 345	Lieutenant Ragaine, J.

XI GROUPEMENT (ST. CHAUMOND)

COMMANDANT	Chef de Battalion HERLAUT
OFFICERS ADJOINTS	Capitaine Rihouet
	Lieutenant Phillippon
	Lieutenant Riboulet
	Med. A-M. Cavaillez
A.S. 34:	Capitaine Deloncle
A.S. 35:	Capitaine Balland

	<u>IV GROUPEMENT (SCHNEIDER)</u>
COMMANDANT	Chefs d'Escadrons CHANOINE C.M.M.
OFFICERS ADJOINTS	Capitain Gignoux C.M.J.
	Lieutenant Marcel L
	Sous-Lieutenant Dupont L.H.R.
	Medec Major Bernes-Lasserre
A.S. 14:	Capitaine Liscoat
A.S. 17:	Capitaine de Sainte-Pereuse E.R.J.

304th American Brigade at St. Mihiel

HEADQUARTERS 304th BRIGADE

November 12, 1918.

OPERATIONS

Of the 304th Tank Brigade, September 12th to 15th, 1918.

ST. MIHIEL SALIENT

1. <u>RECONNAISSANCE.</u>

On the 20th of August Lieutenant Colonel Patton, commanding 304th Brigade, received orders from General Headquarters, attaching the 304th Brigade to the First Army for temporary duty.

A complete reconnaissance on the front included in the 5th Corps[21] area between VERDUN, HAUDIOMONT,[22] VILLE-EN-WOEVRE, HERNEMONT ROAD and COMBRES was made.

It was determined that Tanks could be employed in this sector from the VERDUN, HAUDIOMONT, VILLE-EN-WOEVRE, HERNEMONT ROAD south to TRESAUVAUX on a 5-kilometer front.

These reports were submitted to Chief of Staff, First Army, August 23rd, 1918.

Special Orders 120, Headquarters First Army, A.E.F. September 3rd, 1918, relieved the 304th Brigade from duty with the 5th Corps and attached the 304th Brigade to the 4th Corps[23] for duty.

A complete reconnaissance was made in the area from BOUCONVILLE to BOIS DE LA HAZELLE (included) from September 3rd, 1918, to completion of the operation.

It was determined that Tanks could be employed in this sector between ETANG DE LAMBERINOT and the BENEY, PANNES, ESSEY, BOYAUDEE[24] BOUFFONS ROAD.

---

[21] The V Corps.
[22] Spelled "Haudimont" in main report.
[23] IV Corps.
[24] "Boyaudee Bouffons Road" as typed in original report. More likely name of road is "Boyau des Bouffons"

These reports were submitted to Chief of Staff, First Army September 7th, 1918.

2. <u>ORGANIZATION OF THE COMMAND OF THE 304th BRIGADE.</u>

Pursuant to Special Orders 120, Headquarters, First Army, A.E.F., September 3rd, 1918, and Special Orders 135, Headquarters, First Army A.E.F. September 5th, 1918, the 304th Tank Brigade Commanded by Lieutenant Colonel Patton, consisting of the 344th Battalion (Major Brett), the 345th Battalion (Captain Compton), the 14th and 17th Groups French Tanks (Major Chanoine) were attached to the 4th Army Corps, American Expeditionary Forces for operations in the St. Mihiel Salient.

3. <u>TRANSPORTATION OF TANK UNITS.</u>

The 14th and 17th Groups French Tanks arrived at BOIS DE LA REIMS on the night of September 7th-8th. Portions of the 344th and 345th Battalions arrived on the nights of September 9th-10th, 10th-11th, and 11th-12th, the last company detrained east of ANSAUVILLE 3:15 a.m. on the morning of September 12th and proceeding directly into action.[25]

Each battalion was loaded on two trains (one and a half companies per train).

Frequent delays and sidetracking of trains prevented their arrival long enough prior to the attack to allow time for minor adjustments to the Tanks and give the men much rest.

It was further necessary to detrain Tanks at places other than those selected due to the blocking of railway traffic. Hence longer routes had to be selected which necessarily made use of short spaces of roads and at time temporarily blocked road traffic. Where roads had to be used by Tanks, G3 - 4th Corps issued orders covering their movement.

4. <u>GENERAL CONDITIONS.</u>

---

[25] Patton wrote to his wife Beatrice on September 16, 1918, "Then we started to detrain and that was awful. For 4 nights the French made every mistake they could, sending trains to the wrong place or not sending them at all. The last company of the 327 Battalion detrained at 3:15 a.m. and marched right into action." Martin Blumenson, <u>The Patton Papers 1885-1940</u> (Boston: Houghton Mifflin Company, 1972), p. 581.

The first American Army had as its intention the reduction of the ST. MIHIEL SALIENT. This was to be executed out by two simultaneous attacks; one from south to north executed by the 1st and 4th Army Corps[26] and the other from west to east by the 5th Army Corps. The two attacks were to meet at THILLOT-SOUS-LES-COTES.

The 1st Army Corps[27] was to attack on the front PERE HILARION FARM (inc) to LIGNY (inc).

The initial attack was to be made by three divisions of Infantry in the front line, from left to right the 2nd, 6th and 90th Divisions. The 2nd and 5th Divisions were to attack in brigade column, each division to have at the outset two battalions in the front line. Pace of attack 100 meters in four minutes. Final objective, first phase, to be reached at H plus 6 hours. Orders were then to be given for further objectives.

The 4th Army Corps[28] was to attack on the front Linsy [sic] (inc) HILL 230 and RICHECOURT (inc).

The attack was to be carried out by the three divisions in the front line; left to right the 1st, 42nd and 89th Divisions. Rate of progress 100 meters in four minutes. The final objective of the first phase was to be reached at H plus 6 hours. Orders for the 2nd phase were to follow.

5. DISTRIBUTION AND PLAN OF ATTACK OF TANK UNITS 4th ARMY CORPS.

The 14th and 17th Groups of French Schneiders and the 345th Battalion less 16 Tanks were assigned to operate in the sector of the 42nd Division.

Position of readiness:- South edge of BOIS DE LA HAZELLE.
Point of departure on D-1 night:- East edge of BOIS DE REMIERES.

The 344th Battalion was assigned to operate in the sector of the 1st Division.

Position of readiness:- North and FAUX BOIS DE NAUGINSARD.
Position of departure on D-1 night:- North XIVRAY-ET-MARVOISIN.

---

[26] The I and IV Corps.
[27] The I Corps.
[28] The IV Corps.

The repair and salvage was established at MENIL-LA-TOUR. On D plus 1 day the repair and salvage moved to BOIS DE LA HAZELLE.

6. OPERATIONS.

Plans for Operations Beginning September 12th

<u>345th Battalion:</u> The battalion was directed to attack between the eastern edge of BOIS DE REMIERES and western edge of BOIS DE LA SONNARD in the direction of ESSEY. With two companies in the front echelon, each company having two platoons in the front line and one in support, the third company in each battalion formed the battalion reserve. Owing to the heavily entrenched nature of the terrain, the Tanks were to follow the Infantry until the TRANCHEE DES HOUBLONS had been passed. Then [the Tanks were] to precede the Infantry in the attack on ESSEY and PANNES, should conditions permit the passage of the RUPT DE MAD and the MADINE.

Owing to the width of the trenches and the mud the Tanks had great difficulty in progressing and came under heavy shell fire while crossing the TRANCHEE DES HOUBLONS. Here two Tanks were put out of action by direct hits. The five leading Tanks of this battalion entered the town of ESSEY with the Infantry, and finding the bridge intact proceeded on the south side of the road in the direction of PANNES.

At PANNES the leading Tank entered the town in advance of the Infantry, passed through it and took the road towards BENEY capturing the town of PANNES and turning over to the Infantry 30 German soldiers. This Tank then proceeded in advance of the Infantry in the direction of BENEY. But as the Infantry battalion on the right had not come up, the Infantry at PANNES could not advance and the Tank was recalled.

The remaining four Tanks had by this time come up, and at 12:30 they advanced a second time on BENEY. But as the Infantry at PANNES had orders to advance in the direction of BOIS DE THIAUCOURT, the Tanks, after getting within 400 meters of BENEY, were directed to change direction to the northwest to precede the Infantry. When the Infantry halted on the line of its objective the Tanks withdrew toward PANNES and at 2:00 o'clock these five

Tanks were reinforced by two additional Tanks and advanced preceding the Infantry to the woods northeast of BENEY.

In this operation they drove out machine guns and overran one battery of 77's in the town. At the close of this operation the Tanks returned to PANNES to refill with gas and oil and pass the night there.

Rallying point: September 12th PANNES

Operations of the Schneider Tanks: These Tanks were attached to the left of 83rd Brigade of the 42nd Division.

The 14th Company was allotted to the right Regiment, the 165th.

The 17th Company was allotted to the left Regiment, the 166th.

One section allotted to each attacking battalion and one section in regimental reserve, or readiness BOIS DE LA HAZELLE positions.

Owing to the width of the trenches the Schneiders were unable to precede the Infantry, but followed the first wave closely as far as MAIZERAIS, when they halted in accordance with orders. While approaching MAIZERAIS one Tank was struck by a 150 shell and 15 men were killed and wounded.

Operations of the 344th Battalion with the 1st Division: One platoon of this battalion attacked the SAILLANT DU HAREM to the east of the RUPT DE MAD and succeeded in cutting the wire in front of this salient in advance of the Infantry. The remaining Tanks operating to the west of the river moved between RICHECOURT and the river in the direction of LAHAYVILLE and then against the machine guns in the BOIS DE RATE.

A great many Tanks were struck in the trenches, but 25 reached the town of NONSARD, which they entered in advance of the Infantry silencing machine guns in the church steeple and attacking some machine guns and some 77mm guns along the eastern edge of the BOIS DE RATE and the BOIS QUART DE RESERVE.

Rallying point September 12th on RUPT DE MAD at Point 356, 6-337.8.

Owing to the muddy nature of the ground and the number and width of the trenches, the Tanks used up their gasoline three times faster than was expected, and were all out of gas by 3:00 p.m. September 12th. Some additional gas was taken up to them by sleds in the afternoon of September

12th. Three trucks loaded with gas which attempted to move to ESSEY on the FLIREY-ESSEY road were stopped by the Military Police at FLIREY and not allowed to proceed until 2:00 p.m. September 13th. This fact materially hampered the operations of the Tanks on the morning of the 13th.

Liaison: Liaison officers at the 1st and 42nd Divisions and 4th Army Corps message centers.

A French speaking soldier at the pigeon cote.

Liaison with all units was affected by motorcycle, telephone, runner, pigeon and visual signals. See appended diagram.

Brigade Reserve: One platoon of five Tanks left the Infantry parallels of departure at H-hour in the vicinity of the BOYAU DE LA VERRIERES - BEAUMONT and moved north against the south point of the SAILLANT DU HAREM east of the river. These Tanks were to neutralize machine gun fire and join the remainder of the reserve when it reached the point.

The remainder of the reserve left its point of readiness at H plus 30 minutes, following in rear of the 344th Battalion. They were to keep 2,000 meters in rear of the leading elements of the 344th Battalion.

The formation of both the 344th and the 345th Battalions was in a depth of at least three lines. Where ground permitted this was to be done by placing two companies in the front echelon, each company having two platoons in the front line and one in support; the third company in each battalion forming the battalion reserve.

Supplies: Main supply dump was at MENIL-LA-TOUR. All supplies gasoline, rations etc., were drawn from the main dump and brought forward to advance dumps established at the points of readiness by motor trucks. The supplies were carried forward during the operations by sleds hauled by Tanks and motor trucks. The motor trucks used roads as designated on the 4th Corps circulation map.

Artillery Preparation: Smoke shells to be fired mixed in the barrage along edge of woods and of observation posts.

Ridges, especially the two spurs east and west of MAIZERAIS, screened by smoke.

Batteries to be detailed for fugitive targets, anti-Tank guns etc.

The Attack: The attack opened on the 12th of September at 5:00 a.m. after four hours of artillery preparation.

The 344th Battalion, 345th Battalion and the 14th and 17th Groups of French Tanks advanced to the attack at H-hour.

Operations on September 13th

Fifteen Tanks of the 344th Battalion and 22 Tanks of the 14th and 17th French Groups arrived just south of ST. BENOIT by noon. Here they remained in position the remainder of that day. During the afternoon 15 additional Tanks of the 345th Battalion arrived at ST. BENOIT.

Gas for the 344th Battalion did not arrive until 2:00 p.m. September 13th. Upon its arrival Tanks were filled and moved through NONSARD to VIGNEULLES, where 50 Tanks arrived at 12:00 midnight.

Operations on September 14th

As the Tanks of the 344th Battalion were unable to gain touch with the 1st Division it was decided to move through ST. MAURICE on WOEL in the hope of finding the Division along the WOEL-ST. BENOIT ROAD, so it was known that part of our front line rested along this road.

At 9:00 a.m. the Tanks arrived 2 kilometers west of WOEL where the commanding officer was informed that the Germans had just been driven out of WOEL and that this town was held by a platoon of 20 French Infantry. A message was sent to the Commanding Officer, 1st Division requesting instructions and an officer's patrol was sent into the woods to the south to attempt to regain touch with the 1st Division, or some portion of the 4th Army Corps.

In the meantime the trucks with gas were brought up, the Tanks refilled and the men fed. During this operation the truck train was attacked by hostile airplanes and one soldier was wounded by a bomb fragment through the right arm. No more having arrived at 12:00 noon, it was decided to send a patrol of three Tanks and five dismounted men to WOEL and thence 2 kilometers down the road in the direction of ST. BENOIT.

At 1:30 p.m. the officer in command of this patrol reported the town clear of the enemy and that he was returning. At 2:00 p.m. he was attacked just south of WOEL by a battalion of Infantry and a battery of 77's and at least eight machine guns. He sent a runner to the battalion stating his situation and that he was attacking.

Five Tanks were sent to his assistance arriving at 2:30. These eight Tanks unsupported by Infantry attacked the enemy and drove them to JONVILLE destroying five machine guns and driving the enemy away from a battery of 77's. In attempting to attack these guns to the rear of the Tanks two officers and four men were wounded by shrapnel fire and the attempt to carry off the guns abandoned.

The Tanks returned to the battalion 2 kilometers west of WOEL. At this time the enemy started to register on the location of the battalion with 150's and as the commanding officer had ascertained that he was at least two miles in front of the Infantry line, it was decided to withdraw to ST. MAURICE.

Operations on September 15th

At 9:00 p.m. September 14th all Tanks received orders to withdraw in view of concentrating at the BOIS DE LA HAZELLE. This operation was successfully completed by all Tanks with the exception of three French and two American Tanks, which were partially destroyed by direct hits. The Tanks were safely concentrated in the BOIS DE LA HAZELLE by the night of September 16th, 1918. All movements were made at night. The 344th Battalion moved 25 kilometers.

7. <u>TACTICAL CONCLUSIONS.</u>

Owing to the fact of the enemy's failure at serious resistance the full value of the Tanks was not susceptible of demonstration. In spite of very serious obstacles of terrain the Tanks were in a position to aid the Infantry and would have done so had such assistance been necessary. As it was, the

Tanks entered the towns of NONSARD, PANNES, and BENEY ahead of the Infantry and captured the town of JONVILLE unaided by any Infantry whatever.

          G. S. PATTON, JR.
          Colonel, Tank Corps.
          Commanding 304th Brigade.

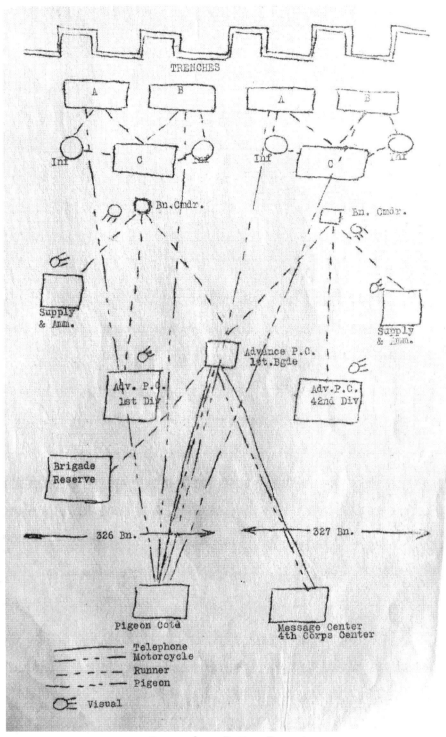

Image from Patton Report.

LOSSES IN PERSONNEL
FROM 12TH TO 16TH OF SEPTEMBER, 1918

Groups & Battalions	Groups & Companies	OFFICERS Killed	OFFICERS Wounded	MEN Killed	MEN Wounded	TOTAL
4TH HEAVY BATTALION	14th GROUP	0	2/E	1/E	8/E	11
	17th GROUP	0	1/E	2/I	2/E	5
344th BATTALION	HQS. CO.	0	0	0	0	0
	CO. A.	0	1	1	2	4
	CO. B.	0	0	0	1	1
	CO. C.	0	0	0	0	0
345th BATTALION	HQS. CO.	0	0	1	0	1
	CO. A.	0	0	0	0	0
	CO. B.	0	0	0	2	2
	CO. C.	0	0	0	0	0

/E Indicates Outside /I Indicates Inside

LOSSES IN MATERIEL
FROM 12TH TO 16TH OF SEPTEMBER, 1918

Groups & Battalion	Groups & Companies	Number of tanks in action	Number of tanks in action	Number of direct hits	Number of tanks out of action for other reasons	Number of tanks fit for action Sept. 16, 1918
4th HEAVY BATTALION	14th Group	17		1	6	10
	17th Group	13		0	1	12
344th BATTALION	HQS. CO.					
	CO. A.	72		0	4 Ditched	69
	CO. B.					
	CO. C.					
345th BATTALION	HQS. CO.	72		0	14 Mechanical trouble	68
	CO. A.					
	CO. B.					
	CO. C.					

Image from Patton Report.

1st French Brigade at St. Mihiel

GRAND QUARTIER GENERAL
des Armees du Nord
et du Nord-Est

G.Q.G., le 25 Aout 1918.

ARTILLERIE D'ASSAUT.

No. 9903.

NOTE DE SERVICE

Le Lieutenant-Colonel WAHL, Commandant la 1st Brigade d'A.S. est designe pour prendre le commandement de toutes les Unites d'A.S. francaises qui pourraient etre mises prochainement a la disposition de l'armee Americaine.

En ce qui concerne l'emploi de l'A.S. Francaise, le Lieut. Colonel WAHL sera place sous les ordres du General Commandant l'AS Americaine, tout en continuant a assurer le commandement de Centre de MAILLY-POIVRES.

Le Lieutenant DUBOIN, Officier de Liaison entre le General ESTIENNE, Commandant l'A.S. Francaise et le General ROCKENBACH, Commandant l'A.S. Americaine, se rendra a partir du 29 Aout aupres du General ROCKENBACH et assurera la liaison entre cet Officer General et le Lieutenant-Colonel WAHL.

LE GENERAL COMMANDANT l'A.S.

ESTIENNE.

DESTINATAIRES:

MM. le Lieut. Col. WAHL, cdt. la 1º Brig. A.S.
le General ELLIS,
le General ROCKENBACH,
le Lieutenant DUBOIN,
le General Cdt en Chef l'Armee Franc.   ) a titre de
Le Marechal Cdt. les armees alliees.   ) comptre-rendu.

Image of first page of Wahl Report.

Translation from A2c. No. 1552 (MKS)

ASSAULT ARTILLERY   G.H.Q., September 23, 1918
1st BRIGADE
STAFF
No. 2184/O.

OPERATIONS OF THE 1st U.S. ARMY from SEPTEMBER 12-15, 1918
(St. Mihiel Salient)

I. RECONNAISSANCES.

August 17 Colonel Wahl, commander of the 1st Assault Artillery Brigade, received from the general commanding Assault Artillery, the order to execute reconnaissance on the front, between the VERDUN-ETAIN ROAD and PONT-A-MOUSSON.

The Chiefs of Battalion Mare and Peraldi-Ficrella are appointed to make these reconnaissances, which are carried out from August 18 to 22.

Major Peraldi studied the sector located between the MOSELLE and APREMONT. He reached the conclusion that the use of Tanks in two unwooded draws, opening here and there in the MORT-MARE WOODS, was possible.

Major Mare studied the sector located between APREMONT and the VERDUN-ETAIN road. He concluded that Tanks could be utilized in but two or three narrow draws, whose width would be considerably diminished by several days of bad weather.

The reports were addressed, August 24, to the general commanding Assault Artillery.

II. ORGANIZATION OF THE COMMAND OF ASSAULT ARTILLERY.

A note from the general commanding Assault Artillery, dated August 25, 1918, appointed Colonel Wahl, commanding the 1st Tank Brigade, commander of all units of French Assault Artillery which could shortly be put at the disposition of the American Army.

Lieutenant Colonel Dupoin, of the Assault Artillery Staff, was appointed to assure Liaison between Colonel Wahl and Brigadier General Rockenbach, U.S.A., Commander of American Assault Artillery.

III. <u>TRANSPORTATION OF ASSAULT ARTILLERY UNITS.</u>

Entrainments

September 5, order was given to the XIIIth, XIVth, and XVth B.C.L. of the 505th Regiment of Assault Artillery, to the 14th and 17th Groups of Assault Artillery, and to the S.R.R., 102, of the 505th Regiment Assault Artillery (Grouping IV) to prepare their entrainment for the following dates:

XIIIth B.C.L. at the POIVRES SPUR in two trains September 6.
XIVth B.C.L. at MAILLY-LE-CAMP in two trains September 6 and 7.
XVth B.C.L. at the POIVRES SPUR in two trains September 8.
Assault Artillery 14, Assault Artillery 17, and Assault Artillery 102 at the POIVRES SPUR in two trains September 6 and 7.

The entrainments took place at the dates fixed upon, with variable delays which were not the fault of the Assault Artillery. Three battalions and a half group to be taken away in a short delay, it was necessary to entrain one of the battalions at MAILLY-LE-CAMP.

The POIVRES SPUR is slight, and of insufficient capacity for an entrainment of this importance. Manoeuvres are long and difficult, the majority of the entrainments are made at night. This experience has shown that, under these conditions, a delay of six hours in entrainment must be estimated for each train. The reduction in the number of cars is anticipated, on demand of the Regulating Committee, in view of the lack of rolling stock. In consequence the echelon on wheels going over ground, it has been possible considerably to reduce the demand for material.

Each battalion was entrained in two hours (one company, one half per train). Makeup of the trains:

    1 car of 1st class.
    3 cars of 3rd class.
    8 covered cars.
    15 flat cars of 15 T.
    18 flat cars of 10 T.

Grouping XI, composed of Assault Artillery 34, 35 and 105 was entrained at MARTIGNY in three trains, be [sic] care of the commander of the Provisory Grouping of St. Chaumond.

Detrainments

XIIIth B.C.L. – Detrainment prepared for at RUPPES. On account of delays the two trains arrive simultaneously at the destination point. In order to set fire the material [sic] as soon as possible, one of the trains is pushed to PUNEROT, and the battalion detrains at once: one train at RUPPES and one at PUNEROT September 7. The battalion is intended to manoeuver with the attacking units of the American Infantry.

XIVth B.C.L. – is to detrain in the VILLERS-EN-HAYE WOODS. Following orders from the American authorities, the companies first detrain at RAUGEVAL September 8. It is possible to obtain a counter-order permitting re-entrainment the same day. September 9 the trains are blocked at the station of the BOYER FARM on account of the crowded tracks and the derailing of a train of heavy artillery. The battalion can detrain the 9th at 6:00 p.m. in the VILLERS-EN-HAYE WOODS. The morning of the 10th it assembles in the PUVENELLE WOODS.

XVth B.C.L. – Detrains September 9, at 2:00 p.m. in the VILLERS-EN-HAYE WOODS. Assembly in the PUVENELLE WOODS the 10th.

Grouping IV – Detrains at the LEOVAL FARM (4 kilometers west of MENIL-LA-TOUR) September 8. The S.R.R. 102 encamps at MENIL-LA-TOUR.

Grouping XI. – Detrains in the RAPPE WOODS: September 7, for 34th Assault Artillery. The S.R.R. 105 encamps in the NOYETTE[29] FARM (south of SAIZERAIS – SAIZERAIS-LIVERDUN ROAD).

XIIIth B.C.L. – The manoeuvres are ended. The battalion detrains at RUPPES, September 7, and detrains at the ROMAN ROAD, September 11, at (1500 meters northwest of ROSIERES-EN-HAYE).

IV. GENERAL CONDITIONS OF THE OPERATION.

The 1st U.S. Army has for its orders the reduction of the St. Mihiel Salient, by two simultaneous attacks: the one to the south - north, led by the 1st and 4th U.S. Army Corps,[30] the other to the west - east, led by the 5th U.S. Army Corps.[31] The two attacks will unite at THILLOT-SOUS-LES-COTES. The 1st Army Corps will attack on the front: PERE HILARION FARM (included) to LIMEY (included). The first attack is made with the 3rd Infantry Division in the first line, from left to right: 2nd Infantry Division, 5th Infantry Division, 90th Infantry Division. The 2nd and 5th Infantry Divisions will attack in brigade columns; each Infantry division will at first have two battalions in the first line. Gait of march 100 meters in four minutes. Objective of first phase to be attained at H1 6.[32]

Orders will be given for later objectives.

The battalion leader Mare, Major of the 505th Regiment of Assault Artillery, is appointed to take command of the Assault Artillery of the 1st U.S. Army Corps, composed as follows:

XIIIth B.C.L.
XIVth B.C.L.
XVth B.C.L.
Grouping XI (Assault Artillery 34-35-S.R.R. 105).

---

[29] Also spelled "Nayette" in this document.
[30] The I and IV Corps.
[31] The V Corps.
[32] H1 6 is how it is typed in the Report. Note that it conflicts with the next similar reference, this time H 1 6.

The 4th Army Corps will attack on the VIMY front (excluded) HILL 230 and RICHECOURT (included). Objectives (see map attached).[33]

The attack is made by the 3rd Infantry Division in line, from left to right: 1st Infantry Division, 42nd Infantry Division, 89th Infantry Division. Gait of march: 100 m. in four minutes. The objective of the first phase will be attained at H 1 6.[34] Orders will follow for the second phase.

Lieutenant Colonel Patton, commanding the 1st U.S. Assault Artillery Brigade,[35] takes command of the Assault Artillery of the 4th U.S. Army Corps, composed as follows:

Grouping IV (Assault Artillery 14-17 S.R.R. 102) Major Chanoine B.C.L.U.S.

V. DISTRIBUTION AND PLANS FOR ENGAGEMENT OF ASSAULT ARTILLERY UNITS U.S. ARMY CORPS.

The XI Grouping is placed at the disposal of the 1st U.S. Army Corps. Command Post: SAIZERAIS.

It will detach a Group (Assault Artillery 34) to the 5th U.S. Infantry Division, a Group (Assault Artillery 35) to the 2nd U.S. Infantry Division. Assembly point: USURE WOODS (east of NOVIANT). Points of Delay: (at J-1). Assault Artillery 34: LAMPE WOODS, northwest of MAMEY. Assault Artillery 36: BOUCHOT WOODS northwest of ST. JACQUES.

The XIIIth B.C.L. is at the disposal of the 2nd U.S. Infantry Division. Assembly point: HAYES WOODS northeast of NOVIANT. Temporary position: At (J-1) BOUCHOT WOODS.

The XIVth B.C.L. is at the disposition of the 5th U.S. Infantry Division. Assembly point: southwest PUVENELLE WOODS. Temporary position: at (J-1) LAMPE WOODS.

---

[33] While various maps are referenced in the archived *Rockenbach Report* located at Carlisle Barracks, only one is stored there with the *Report*. Its image is reproduced and included with the supporting documents under "301st Battalion with the British E.F."
[34] See above footnote.
[35] 304th (1st Provisional) Tank Brigade.

The XVth B.C.L. (Army Corps Reserve). Assembly point: southwest edge of PUVENELLE WOODS. Temporary position: south of MAMEY. The S.R.R. 105 will be installed at the NAYETTE[36] FARM (SAIZERAIS-LIVERDUN ROAD).

The mission of Groups 34 and 35 is:

1. To aid in the surprise of the first line by advancing against this line ahead of the Infantry to make passages in the intervals of defenses.

2. To assist the progress of the Infantry (as possibilities for passage occur, into the trenches made ready by the Engineers), as far as the first German line of resistance (trenches of the EUZEVIN, the FOUR and the RAPPE WOODS). The Infantry division first reaching a brigade column, each group being attached to a brigade.

The batteries will be evenly distributed over each brigade front to assure the opening of breaches on the entire front.

The XIIIth and XIVth B.C.L. will intervene only when the first system of trenches has been passed and then beyond the first line of resistance, in the direction of THIAUCOURT, for the XIIIth B.C.L. and of VIEVILLE, for the XIVth B.C.L.

A company is attached to each regiment attacking. A company is attached to each reserve brigade.

Liaisons:

Major of B.C.L. of Command Post of Infantry Division.

Major of Group at Command Post of Brigade.

Major of Company at Command Post of Regiment.

The sections will detach a noncommissioned officer and a man speaking English to the battalion commander to which they are adjoined.

A wireless car with a battalion. A wireless car at the liaison center of the Infantry division (command post of attacking brigade).

Reserve battalions [sic] the XVth B.C.L. (Light Tank Battery), will march at the head of the first elements of the reserve Infantry division. Progress by battalions on the axis of liaison of the Army Corps: MAMEY–REQUIEVILLE–LA

---

[36] Also spelled "Noyette" in this document. However, reference to " Camp Nayette, near Saizerais, headquarters of the Sixth Corps..." can be found online at
http://freepages.military.rootsweb.ancestry.com/~cacunithistories/58tharty.htm

GRISIERE FARM. Study on the map and photographs the possibilities of engagement on:
- a) FONTAINE WOODS, PRENY.
- b) SAULNY.
- c) XAMMES, CHANEY.

Study also the means of intervening against enemy attacks proceeding from the VILLERS-SOUS-PRENY and PRENY ravines.

The Battalion Commander of the XVth B.C.L. will remain at the A.C. Post of command during the attack. Post of command of Assault Artillery of 1st U.S.A.C.

Post of Command of the Army Corps – SAIZERAIS.

Supplies will be advanced on the liaison axis of each Infantry division and, for the XVth B.C.L., on the liaison axis of the Army Corps. Gasoline supply for units from II to MENIL-LA-TOUR.

Smoke generating shells on the barrage and observations.

Reserve batteries to fight anti-Tank guns.

U.S.A.C. [sic].

The 42nd U.S. Infantry Division attacks first with two brigades beside it.

Grouping IV is attached to the left Brigade, 83rd.

The 83rd Brigade has its two regiments beside it (165 and 166 U.S. Infantry Regiments). Assault Artillery 14 is attached to the regiment to the right. One battery attached to each attacking battalion; one battery in reserve per regiment. Temporary position: HAZELLE WOODS.

The batteries will go to their starting position, take advantage of the noise of preparation.

The car will rejoin the Infantry as soon as the arrangement of the terrain will permit, and will assist it as far as RUPT DE MAD. While waiting for passages to be made they will rally in the ravine south of MAIZERAIS.

They will then intervene between RUPT DE MAD and MADINE; will await the moment to cross to the south of PANNES and will reassemble at the end of the day, between PANNES and HILL 243 (northwest of PANNES). Command post of IV Groupement:[37] 83rd Brigade.

---

[37] Translated "grouping" in some of the American reports.

Protection by the Artillery: Smoke generating shells will be fired by the Artillery on the crests, especially on the two spurs to the east and west of MAIZERAIS.

VI. EXECUTION OF FIRST ATTACK.

12th of September

1st Army Corps, U.S., 5th Division Infantry U.S. Assault Artillery 34:- The 2nd and 3rd Batteries of the group arrive at the division post at 1:00. The first battery arrives at 5:30.

At the H (?) [sic][38] Hour two Tanks preceded the Infantry up to the enemy's position, making breaches in the wire entanglements.

The other cars had a breakdown, as a result of the bad condition of the ground, and advance with difficulty.

At 17 o'clock,[39] six available Tanks go to a waiting position in the SAULX WOODS.

At the hour H (?) [sic] the Assault Artillery Companies 340 and 341 present themselves to the division post (P.D.) Assault Artillery 342 is in reserve of the Infantry division in the LAMPE WOODS.

Assault Artillery 340 loses a Tank on a mine at the entrance of the SAULX WOODS.

At the end of the day the situation of the Tanks is the following:
2 Tanks at southeast end of HEICHE WOODS.
5 Tanks at the north border of SAULX WOODS.
5 Tanks at the south border of SAULX WOODS.

The Assault Artillery 341 leaves at H (?) [sic] o'clock, is quickly passed by the Infantry, and arrives, at the end of the day, with 11 Tanks, near the route from REGNIEVILLE to THIAUCOURT.

2nd Infantry Division U.S.: Assault Artillery 35: The Assault Artillery 35 was assembled at the division post, only at 7:00 a.m. September 12. The men

---

[38] The *Report* states "H (?)," ergo my [sic] notation.
[39] Assume this means 1700 hours.

necessary for the establishment of the parks were not sent in time by the staff of the 2nd U.S. Infantry Division.

The terrain was in disorder, the trenches could be passed only with difficulty. The earth was muddy.

Nine Tanks left at 7 o'clock. Only two arrived at 17 o'clock at the south end of HEICHE WOOD. One Tank blew up on a mine on the east edge of FOUR WOODS. All the others had a breakdown.

XIIIth B.C.L.:- The units of the 13th B.C.L. are at the division post, September 12, 5:00 a.m.

The 339 Company receives at H (?) [sic] o'clock orders to go to the north of LIMEY, where it remains all day without taking any part in the section.

At H (?) [sic] o'clock, the 337th and 338th Companies go ahead. The passage of the trenches is difficult, the ground is very slippery.

The Infantry, experiencing no resistance, passes quickly ahead of the Tanks, which have not [sic] to intervene. At 15:30 o'clock, the Infantry Division gives the Tanks orders to reassemble at the south of HEICHE WOODS.

The 338th Company presents itself in its entirety, while the 337th Company has left half of its Tanks in the trenches with a breakdown.

Assault Artillery in Reserve of the 1st Army Corps:- The 15th B.C.L. in reserve of the Army Corps at the end of the day goes from the valley southwest of REGNIEVILLE to FOUR WOODS, where it takes up its station.

4th Army Corps U.S.A., 83rd U.S. Brigade - IV Groupement:- The 4th Groupement put at the disposition of the 83rd U.S. Brigade. (Assault Artillery 14 detailed with the 165th Infantry U.S. and Assault Artillery 17 detailed with the 166th Infantry U.S.). Departure at 4 o'clock.

The Assault Artillery No. 14 acts on the HAUBLANS TRENCHES (east of BAUSSANT) and neutralizes the machine guns of the village which is then occupied by the American Infantry. The 17 Assault Artillery neutralizes the machine guns of MAIZERAIS and of the brow of the hill southeast of the village, which were hindering the progress of the Infantry.

The village of ESSEY is given to the Infantry by the Tanks, with 40 prisoners.

A Tank of command of the 17 Assault Artillery received a direct hit by a shell east of MAIZERAIS.

At the end of the day the groups take up their station to the north of MAIZERAIS.

13th of September

1st Army Corps, U.S., 5th Division Infantry U.S.:-
Assault Artillery 34 was not engaged.

14th B.C.L.: The Battalion is grouped at HEICHE WOODS, where 19 Tanks are reassembled.

2nd Infantry Division U.S.: Assault Artillery 35:- In the morning, the command post of the group puts four Tanks at the disposal of the Infantry which continues its attack.

One Tank has a track breakdown. The three others reach the CHAREY ROAD, 800 meters north of XAMMES and neutralize the machine guns in the ravine 1 kilometer northwest of XAMMES and at the west edge of RUPT WOODS.

The Tanks regain the position they left.

At the end of the day the group [sic] to the crossroads, JAULNEY-VIEVILLE-EN-HAYE, to parry a counterattack which did not take place. They return to the south of HEICHE WOODS.

XIIIth B.C.L.:- Assault Artillery 337 and 339, without change.

The 339th Assault Artillery receives at 9 o'clock, orders to go to THIAUCOURT, where it takes up a position of waiting south of the village.

Assault Artillery in Reserve of the 1st Army Corps:– 15th B.C.L. goes from FOUR WOODS to the south edge of HEICHE WOODS.

4th Army Corps U.S.A., 83rd U.S. Brigade:- Bivouac of the groups at ST. BENOIT and at SEBASTOPOL FARM.

14th of September

1st Army Corps, U.S., 5th Division Infantry U.S.:-
Assault Artillery 34: Receives orders to go as reserve of Army corps at the south edge of HEICHE WOODS, where it arrives 3:00 a.m.
14th B.C.L.: Reassembly in HEICHE WOODS.

4th U.S. Army Corps:-
Assault Artillery 35: Reassembles south of HEICHE WOODS.
13th B.C.L.: The battalion receives orders to regroup in HEICHE WOODS. The bottling of the roads is such that the battalion modifies the point where it was to take up its position, and hides in the rectangular woods, situated at the north of GRISIERE FARM.

4th Army Corps U.S. 83rd U.S. Brigade:– Situation unchanged.

15th of September

Regrouping of the Elements of the Assault Artillery:–
Grouping XI in RAPPE WOODS.
XIIIth, XIVth, and XVth B.C.L. in VILLERS-EN-HAYE WOODS.
Grouping IV in HAZELLE WOODS, then at ANSAUVILLE.

Regrouping at End of Operations:– A cipher telegram September 15, 26:10 o'clock from General Headquarters, orders that the Assault Artillery placed at the disposal of the 1st U.S. Army[40] will be regrouped in the zones mentioned hereafter:

Light Tanks: LIONVILLE REGION.
Medium Tanks: DOMEVRE-EN-HAYE.

---

[40] First Army.

After consultation with the Regulating Commission it was prescribed that the points of re-embarkation would be the following:

B.C.L.:	VILLERS-EN-HAYE WOODS.
XI Grouping:	RAPPE WOODS.
IV Grouping:	ANSAUVILLE.

VII. GENERAL REMARKS.

It is very difficult to obtain trains provided with suitable carriages. The flat cars are without lookout boxes and have small dismountable sides. But it frequently happens that they have floors barred with heavy cross beams. The Assault Artillery material and rolling stock suffer likewise on account of this.

Other cars have floor more or less rotten or flattened springs which necessitate enroute a change of cars, which always take a long time.

The defective gearing of a train of the 14th B.C.L. necessitated long movements, whence a delay of six hours in leaving.

A train of the 15th B.C.L. leaves POIVRES, one hour and 30 minutes late, as a result of the derailing of two cars.

The movement of the 13th B.C.L. from RUPPES to the VOIE ROMAINE (ROMAN ROAD) should have had priority. However, by order of the First American Army, many trains of ballast passed before this battalion, encumbering the tracks in such a way that it took 48 hours to go from ROMAINE. It was obliged to go directly to the artillery park without stopping at the (?) [sic] reassembling points.

The 14th B.C. took three days to go from POIVRES to VILLERS-EN-HAYE, for similar reasons.

The outfits arrived very tired at the reassembling points.

VIII. TACTICAL CONCLUSIONS.

1. The transportation and especially the unloading were very faulty. The tracks were encumbered with trains of high power heavy artillery. Poorly constructed, they sometimes crumbled. The trains of ballast increased the confusion. Certain units remained two hours in the train. The result was a loss of time in taking contact, and an extreme fatigue of the personnel.

2. The police of the roads [was] often non-existent, and sometimes without intelligence. For instance, supply trains of gas were stopped on the pretext that only ammunition was authorized to pass.

3. With a view to keeping the secret of the operations, the units were brought up tardily, the plans of the engagement communicated at the last minute, and the verbal information that could be picked up in staff, given with extreme parsimony. The result was difficulty in taking contact with the Infantry units, and a great uncertainty as to the intentions secret [sic]. The units of the Assault Artillery were kept to the front, when the operation was not to take place, and it was very difficult to have them retire.

4. The enemy offered only an insignificant resistance; the Infantry advanced very quickly; the Tanks did not have to take part in the taking of the first position. But if it had been necessary for them to do so they would have been able to act only with very diminished means, by a progression in a terrain, soaked by the rains, and especially, furrowed by defensive preparations four years old. On the other hand, on September 13, the units were in a condition to take part with almost all their means, but the enemy's resistance was always feeble and it seems that the Infantry desirous of keeping the whole glory of the success, had some reluctance about asking for the intervention of the Assault Artillery.

IX. <u>GERMAN ANTI-TANK DEFENSES.</u>

The German anti-Tank defensive preparations in the sector were of [the following] kinds:

1. Troops, covered with camouflaged planks. One Tank of the 337th Assault Artillery fell into one of these. It was quickly gotten out.

2. Mines, which seem much more effective than the preceding method. (The model has been described in a recent information bulletin of the 2nd Army). A Tank of the XIVth B.C.L. was disemboweled and cut in two; the cupola was thrown several meters away; caterpillars, motor lower casing, was broken into many pieces; the driver was killed. A St. Chamond Tank met another of these mines. Only the primer shell exploded. The caterpillar was broken and a reservoir pierced. No accident to personnel. It is to be noticed that a light Tank had just passed over this mine without exploding it. It is

impossible in full combat to avoid these perils. The only means of diminishing the danger seems to have suspected sites heavily bombarded by the Artillery before the attack, so as to explode the majority of the mines beforehand.

    3. Anti-Tank guns were found in various places. On account of the weak resistance of the enemy only passive defensives (mines and pitfalls) were encountered.

X. <u>TECHNICAL CONCLUSIONS.</u>

    1. The rolling stock placed at the disposal of the Assault Artillery units is insufficient. A company has the wherewithal to transport 18 tons, not including the shop in tow. It should transport 23 tons; five without the shop. It needs 5-ton trucks. It would be necessary likewise to borrow one extra vehicle, a small truck and a motor-cycle from the regimental commanders, and two powerful motor-cycles with sidecars, American type, from the grouping and battalion commanders.

    2. The breaking of ventilation belts of belt fasteners [was] frequent (at least 20 per company) during the operations of September 12. These breaks in belts are due to many causes (swelling of the unstretched belt, because of an excessive speed of the motor, involving shock against belts, etc.) However, they can be decreased to a very large degree, by placing exactly in the same plane the two pullies of the ventilator. The experience of the 502nd Regiment of Assault Artillery, and Grouping IV, [sic] as time was lacking before the departure of these units to the Armies.

    3. Getting cars in working order after breakdowns is difficult with present means. Getting a Renault car out of a breakdown with another Renault car is having a breakdown with both. Getting a car out of a breakdown with a Baby Holt would be easier. However, it offers great dangers, the Baby Holt being very noisy and drawing the attention of the enemy. Moreover, this tractor cannot draw it with any large machine. The best solution would be to attach to each battalion two Schneiders, without armament, and their double casing. These cars would transport considerable materiel, including the necessary personnel.

    4. The combat supply is impossible by road. The solution must be sought:

a) By the material of caterpillars. Stripped St. Chamond cars and Schneider cars would be effective here. Lightened and well driven, they would assure gasoline, food and munitions for the first line.

b) Sledges. The type of sledge (two planks placed edge to edge braced with U irons, and turned up at the front), adopted by Grouping II since October 23, 1917, seems to have given excellent results. These sledges can each transport from 200 to 250 litres of gasoline.

5. The telephone material of the regimental staff should be augmented. 20 kilometers of wire should doubtless be enough to assure liaison between regiments and units. A four direction board is insufficient. It would also be necessary to give the regiment a telephone crew similar to that of the Artillery regiment.

Colonel Wahl
Commander of the 1st Assault
Artillery Brigade

1ST (304TH) AMERICAN BRIGADE AT MEUSE-ARGONNE

OPERATIONS REPORT OF THE 1st (304th) TANK BRIGADE[41] FROM NOON SEPTEMBER 26th, 1918, TO NOVEMBER 10, 1918.

Preparations for entering the Meuse-Argonne Offensive by the 1st Brigade, Tank Corps, has been covered by the complete operations report of the 1st Brigade. The initial Tank dispositions were as follows: 344th Battalion leading with one company operating west of the RIVER AIRE and two companies operating east of the RIVER AIRE, between the RIVER AIRE and the STREAM BUANTHE; 345th Battalion in support, disposed in the same manner as the 344th Battalion; 14th and 17th Groups (French) in reserve echelon about 2,000 meters in rear of the leading battalion, operating between the RIVER AIRE and the STREAM BUANTHE.

The Brigade Commander, Lieutenant Colonel George S. Patton, Jr., was wounded early in the first day of attack, September 26th, 1918, and command of the Brigade was assumed by Major Sereno E. Brett, Commanding Officer, 344th Battalion.

September 26th, 1918

Resistance encountered during the morning was very severe, principally from enemy machine guns and artillery fire. The Tanks went forward time after time in an endeavor to clear the way for the Infantry, but in nearly all cases the Infantry did not follow, thereby making the Tank efforts futile. Resistance was particularly strong east of VAUQUOIS HILL, along the edge of the FORET D'ARGONNE and in and around the towns of CHEPPY and VARENNES. The Tanks entered the town of VARENNES at 9:30 in the morning, but the Infantry support did not arrive until 1:30 p.m. During the night, the Tanks operating on the west side of the RIVER AIRE were assembled at BOUREUILLES and those operating east of the RIVER AIRE were assembled in the small patch of woods southwest of CHEPPY. For casualties, see attached consolidated report.

---

[41] The 304th Tank Brigade was redesignated the 1st (Provisional) Tank Brigade "shortly after its formation...although it retained its 304th title in the St. Mihiel offensive." Robert E. Rogge, "304th Tank Brigade: Its Formation and First Two Actions," Armor, July-August 1988, p. 26.

September 27th, 1918

Forty-three American Tanks were out of action due to the action of September 26th. Eleven Tanks supported the advance of the Infantry of the 28th Division on the east edge of the FORET D'ARGONNE, and fought a very severe action throughout the entire day, mostly against pill boxes, of which there was a great number. On the east of the RIVER AIRE there seemed to be no concerted action contemplated on the part of the Infantry, therefore no Tanks entered the fight during the day, except two platoons of Company "A," 344th Battalion, which supported an attack on the plateau north of VERY. During the afternoon the brigade command post was moved back to the COTES D'FORIMONT[42] at the request of the Chief of Staff, 1st Army Corps.[43] Captain Compton was placed in command of all forward units, with command post at VARENNES.

The 14th and 17th Groups (French) 12 Tanks went into action at 5:00 p.m. on a line CHARPENTRY to road 1 kilometer south of SERIEUX FERME. The Tanks entered CHARPENTRY but the Infantry did not follow.

September 28th, 1918

Eighty-Three American Tanks and 12 French Tanks were ready for action in the morning. Their positions were as follows:

Company "C" 344th Battalion: 13 Tanks at CHEPPY.
Company "A" 344th Battalion: 10 Tanks at VERY.
Company "B" & "C" 345th Battalion: 30 Tanks at MONTBLAINVILLE.
Company "A" 345th Battalion and Company "B" 344th Battalion:
     6 Tanks south of MONTBLAINVILLE; 24 Tanks enroute from the rear to VARENNES; 12 Tanks (French) south of CHARPENTRY.

---

[42] Editor's note: Also spelled "de Forimont" in another section of this report.
[43] The I Corps.

Assignment for the day was made on the evening of the 27th, as follows:

28th Division:	15
35th Division:	42 (Including 6 French)
91st Division:	5 (To act as combat liaison group between the 35th and 91st Divisions)
	27 unassigned as Brigade Reserve

The Tanks assigned supported their respective divisions throughout the entire day. The fighting was very severe and a great deal of anti-Tank defense was encountered. Losses among the Tanks and personnel were particularly heavy during the day (see consolidated casualty report attached).

Lack of Infantry support was still very noticeable. During the day the Tanks took the town of APREMONT five times before the Infantry would enter, consolidate and exploit the success. In many instances the Infantry seemed to have forgotten the fire power which they themselves possessed and expected the Tanks to completely obliterate all opposition before they would advance.

The group of French Tanks again attacked CHARPENTRY and did splendid work.

September 29th, 1918

French Tanks commenced to withdraw to the rear in compliance with orders received from First Army during the day.

Fifty-five American Tanks were ready for action in the morning. The repair and salvage units worked throughout the entire night to bring the number of Tanks up to this total. These Tanks were assigned as follows: 15 to the 28th Division; 40 to the 35th Division.

Tanks assigned to the 28th Division, operating on the east edge of the FORET D'ARGONNE developed severe actions with machine guns throughout the day and did splendid execution. Later, during the afternoon, they were ordered to the vicinity of APREMONT to aid in resisting an expected counterattack. Nothing developed during the remainder of the day. During the action in the morning and afternoon, the Tanks encountered severe artillery fire coming from the ridge northwest of APREMONT.

Tanks assigned to the 35th Division, with the exception of an action south of EXERMONT in which 11 Tanks were engaged, did not do much, due to the apparent indifference of the Infantry. Late in the afternoon, the Tanks were called upon to assist in resisting a counterattack directed from the MONTREBEAU WOODS and were ordered to hold the line BAULNY-ECLISFONTAINE. This was done. Tank patrol assisted by Engineers, were established to allow the Infantry to reorganize on the new line. The Tanks were withdrawn after dark.

September 30th, 1918

In compliance with P.O. 61 First Army Corps, September 30th, 1918, all Tanks were withdrawn to reserve positions in the vicinity of BAULNY and CHARPENTRY for the purpose of reorganizing and repairing.

On the morning of September 30th 20 Tanks were dispatched at the request of the 35th Division to assist in resisting a counterattack anticipated north of CHARPENTRY. Nothing developed and the Tanks returned to their reserve position at 1:30 p.m. the same day. During the afternoon five Tanks were dispatched at the request of the 28th Division to patrol northwest of APREMONT to the STREAM CROISETTE. No resistance was encountered and no enemy seen, so the Tanks returned to their reserve positions on completion of their mission.

October 1st, 1918

Sixty-one Tanks reported ready for action. During the evening of September 30th, the 28th Division requested a group of eight Tanks to cooperate with the attack which was to be launched at 6:00 a.m. October 1st. The enemy, however, counterattacked at 5:30 a.m. The Tanks were in place and did frightful execution among the massed ranks of the enemy. Brigadier General Nolan, 28th Division, was on the ground and personally commended the Tank commanders for their valuable work. Summary of Intelligence, 1st Army Corps, dated October 2nd, contains the following, relative to this action: "Prisoners of the 2nd Ludendorff Division state that in the counterattack north of APREMONT they were completely demoralized by our Tanks, as most of the soldiers, as well as most of the officers, had never seen Tanks before. Tanks did very effective work and after having gone through the lines, turned around and came back through them again at the same time inflicting casualties."

A patrol of two Tanks operating on the road APREMONT-LE MENIL FARM encountered slight resistance and returned to their position on reserve on completion of their mission.

Repair and salvage work is being handled in splendid shape by First Lieutenant Thompson, but is becoming more difficult, due to the proximity of the enemy lines to disabled Tanks.

October 2nd, 1918

No action during the day. Tanks were in reserve positions in the vicinity of CHARPENTRY and MONTBLAINVILLE. Repair and salvage work progressed in splendid shape. Several of the men and officer were withdrawn to VARENNES to permit them to gain a little rest.

October 3rd, 1918

Same as October 2nd, 1918

October 4th, 1918

Eighty-nine Tanks ready for action. The disposition for the attack on October 4th was made as follows:

Two companies to the 1st Division (which had replaced the 35th Division).

One company to the 28th Division.

Remaining Tanks were retained in position as brigade reserve until 2:00 p.m., at which time a group of 13 Tanks moved forward in rear of the 1st Division. These were intended for replacements at the end of the day, and did not enter the action.

The Tanks went over the top in advance of the Infantry at H-hour in the morning. The support rendered to the Tanks by the 1st Division was splendid, and this division reported that the Tanks did very effective work. These reciprocal reports no doubt resulted from the excellence of the liaison between the two units. The support given by the 28th Division had also much improved. The artillery fire encountered on this day was particularly accurate and severe. Strong resistance was encountered in the advance in the vicinity of HILL 240 in the sector of the 1st Division and along the edge of the FORET D'ARGONNE in the sector of the 28th Division. Casualties in personnel and equipment were heavy during the day.

October 5th, 1918

Thirty Tanks were ready for action the morning of October 5th. Dispositions were made as follows:

15 to the 1st Division.
15 to the 28th Division.

Neither of the divisions to which Tanks were assigned called for them during the day. Tanks, however, moved up to close support of the divisions, and after dark returned to their positions.

Mechanical difficulties in Tanks are becoming more numerous each day. This is due to the fact that the Tanks have been under severe test, both in the St. Mihiel and the present offensive.

The men and officers are in good spirits.

The "Flu" has caused numerous men and officers to be evacuated and the nightly gassing on the positions around CHARPENTRY has caused a little sickness and inconvenience.

October 6th, 1918

Seventeen Tanks were ready for action on the morning of October 6th, but under direction of the 1st Army Corps they were held in reserve positions.

October 7th, 1918

One company (15 Tanks) was ordered to support the attack of the 28th Division this morning. Only eight Tanks on the west side of the RIVER AIRE were in condition to enter battle and these three [sic] were dispatched. One of these struck a mine and was disabled, but the remaining Tanks reported and were used throughout the day mostly for patrol work.

October 8th, 1918

Twenty-six Tanks ready for action on the morning of October 8th. These were assigned to the 28th and 82nd Divisions, but neither division called them into action during the day, due to the unsuitability of the terrain.

Command post 1st Brigade, Tank Corps, moved from the COTES D'FORIMONT to VARENNES.

The "Flu" is still causing a number of evacuations.

Repair and salvage work was progressing nicely.

Supply and communications have worked perfectly since the beginning of the offensive.

October 9th, 1918

Thirty-five Tanks ready for action on the morning of October 9th. These were placed at the disposal of the 82nd Division, but they were not called for during the day.

October 10th, 1918

No action and no dispositions.

October 11th, 1918

Forty-eight Tanks ready for action on the morning of October 11th. At midnight, October 10th, 23 Tanks left the town of VARENNES to report to the Commanding General, 164th Brigade, 82nd Division, at FLEVILLE. The request had been made for five Tanks, but due to the distance of the run, it was thought advisable to send a much larger number forward in view of the poor mechanical condition of the Tanks. Only three of these reached FLEVILLE and these were rejected by the Commanding General to whom they were to report.

A group of five Tanks ordered to report to the 77th Division at PYLONE reported, but they were not called for during the day.

Letter from the Chief of Tank Corps, dated October 11th, 1918, was received. This letter directed the organization of one Provisional Company, operating 16 Tanks, and having a total of 24 Tanks, 96 men in the Tank crews and the balance of the personnel as provided in the Tank Corps tables of organization. It further directed that on completion of the organization of the Provisional Company the 345th Battalion and other company officers and men, less those attached to the composite company, be withdrawn; also that all Tanks not operating be brought to VARENNES and repaired.

October 12th, 1918

Letter received from the 1st Division commending the work of the 1st Brigade, Tank Corps, while supporting that division from September 29th, 1918 to October 11th, 1918 inclusive.

The details of organizing the Provisional Company were pushed.

October 13th, 1918

On this date the Provisional Company of the 1st Brigade, Tank Corps, was organized with the following organization:

Captain Courtney Barnard, Tank Corps, Commanding
10 Officers (including Captain Barnard)
148 Enlisted Men
159 Total Strength

Equipment:

24 Tanks
1 Dodge Car
4 Trucks
1 Motorcycle, with Sidecar
1 Rolling Kitchen
1 Water Wagon

October 14th, 1918

The 1st Brigade, Tank Corps, less Headquarters Company, 344th Battalion, the 321st R & S Company and the Provisional Company, was directed to withdraw to the 302nd Tank Center, Tank Corps, per S.O. 343, Headquarters, First Army, dated October 14th, 1918.

During the evening of October 14th, the Provisional Company started to march to EXERMONT to be in readiness for action. During the evening the Provisional Company was loaned to the 5th Army Corps by the 1st Army Corps (to which we have been assigned since the commencement of the offensive of September 26th).

The Commanding General, 5th Corps, directed the brigade commander to report to the Commanding General, 42nd Division for instructions. The brigade commander reported immediately to the Commanding General, 42nd Division and learned that he desired to employ the Tanks the following morning between LANDRES-ET-ST. GEORGES and ST. GEORGES.

Plans were rapidly made for their employment and the commanding officer of the Provisional Company [was] notified while the company was still on the road to EXERMONT. Due to the great distance of the march and the grueling speed at which the Tanks were forced to march in order to be in battle position at H-hour, only 10 of the Tanks reached the battle position.

These Tanks just reached their positions to go over the top at H-hour. They progressed into the enemy's trenches, and there ran into what appeared to be the formation of a counterattack. The Infantry did not support the Tanks, so after they had dispersed the enemy, the Tanks returned to EXERMONT.

Units directed to return to the 302nd Center, Tank Corps, by Special Orders 343, First Army, dated October 14th, 1918, left this date by motor truck.

October 16th to October 31st, 1918 (both inclusive)

Operations on large scale did not take place during this period and the Tanks were not called on to take place in any action, and remained in reserve at EXERMONT.

October 17th, 1918

9th Company, 2nd Regiment M.M.S.C., which was attached to the 1st Brigade from the commencement of the offensive, was ordered from CAMP FOURGOUS to VARENNES to assist in the repairs to Tanks.

October 18th, 1918

    Tank situation as follows:
In park and located	89
At EXERMONT	31
Salvaged	1
Total accounted for	121
Unaccounted for	20
Total running	50

October 19th, 1918

    Tank situation as follows:
Accounted for	130
Unaccounted for	11
Running	50

October 20th, 1918

    Tank situation as follows:
Accounted for	133
Unaccounted for	8
Running	53

October 21st, 1918

    Tank situation as follows:
Accounted for	133
Unaccounted for	8
Running	61

October 22nd, 1918

    Tank situation as follows:
Accounted for	133
Unaccounted for	8
Running	62

October 23rd, 1918

> Tank situation as follows:
> Accounted for   137
> Unaccounted for   4
> Running   65

October 24th, 1918

> Tank situation as follows:
> Accounted for   138
> Unaccounted for   3
> Running   65

October 25th, 1918

> Tank situation as follows:
> Accounted for   140
> Unaccounted for   1
> Running   66

October 26th, 1918

> Tank situation as follows:
> Accounted for   140
> Unaccounted for   1
> Running   68

October 27th, 1918

> Tank situation as follows:
> Accounted for   140
> Unaccounted for   1
> Running   68

The ground has been thoroughly reconnoitered for the Tank which is still missing, but no trace of it can be found.

October 28th, 1918

>   Tank situation as follows:
>   Accounted for   140
>   Unaccounted for   1
>   Running   68

October 29th, 1918

>   Tank situation as follows:
>   Accounted for   140
>   Unaccounted for   1
>   Running   72

October 30th, 1918

>   Tank situation as follows:
>   Accounted for   140
>   Unaccounted for   1
>   Running   78

October 31st, 1918

>   Tank situation as follows:
>   Accounted for   140
>   Unaccounted for   1
>   Running   82

The Tank which was missing on this date was never found during the time covered by this report, and it is believed that it was disabled and captured by the enemy or had fallen into the river where it could not be located.

November 1st, 1918

Fifteen Tanks of the Provisional Company this date supported the advance of the 2nd Division on a line between LANDRES-ET-ST. GEORGES and ST. GEORGES. One platoon was directed against the wire in front of and the town of ST. GEORGES. The other two platoons were directed against the wire in front of and the town of LANDRES-ET-ST. GEORGES. The cooperation between the Tanks and the Marines and Infantry was splendid.

The Division gave the Tanks excellent support and local commanders were high in their praise of the work accomplished by the Tanks. The Tanks were later commended for this action in a letter from Major General C. P. Summerall, Commanding General 5th Corps. North of ST. GEORGES three Tanks under command of Lieutenant Callahan, Tank Corps, flanked and put out of action an enemy battery of four 77mm guns.

Tank situation on the evening of November 1st:
Tanks accounted for   140
Tanks unaccounted for   1
Tanks running   67

November 2nd, 1918

The Provisional Company was again assigned to the 2nd Division, but it was not called. It remained in reserve positions in LANDRES-ET-ST. GEORGES.

The 321st R & S Company, in compliance with instructions received from the Chief of Tank Corps, moved from VARENNES to the 302nd Center, Tank Corps, by motor truck.

Reports on Tank situations were hereafter made by the commanding officer of the 3rd Brigade, Tank Corps, who is preparing to relieve the remaining elements of the 1st Brigade.

November 3rd, 1918

Tanks entered no other action until the signing of the Armistice closed hostilities.

The command post of the Provisional Company remained in EXERMONT, but the Tanks were pushed forward in an endeavor to keep up with the Infantry in case they were again needed. Tanks parked in LANDREVILLE during the night of November 3rd-4th.

November 4th, 1918

No change.

November 5th, 1918

No change of station of the Provisional Company. The 331st and 345th Battalions of the 3rd Brigade, Tank Corps, arrived to relieve the remaining elements of the 1st Brigade, Tank Corps.

November 6th, 1918

Command post of the Provisional Company and equipment thereof pushed up to BAYONVILLE during the morning.

November 7th, 1918

No change.

November 8th, 1918

No change.

November 9th, 1918

Personnel of the Provisional Company belonging to the 344th Battalion returned to VARENNES preparatory to returning to the 302nd Center, Tank Corps, in compliance with instructions from the Chief of Tank Corps.

The 3rd Brigade, Tank Corps, relieved the 1st Brigade, Tank Corps, and took over all Tanks.

November 10th, 1918

All remaining elements of the 1st Brigade, Tank Corps, left VARENNES for the 302nd Center, Tank Corps, by motor.

GENERAL

Repair and Salvage

Repair and salvage work in the brigade was particularly well handled by the 321st R & S Company. The work, often under shell fire, of First Lieutenant Jesse L. Thompson and the other officers and men of the 321st R & S Company was highly commendable.

Supply

No difficulty was experienced in supplying the brigade at any time. The supply system was well organized and functioned admirably. The work of First Lieutenant Roswell King, as Acting Brigade Supply Officer, showed merit of the highest order.

Communications

Telephonic communications were established between battalions and brigade and between brigade and divisions and corps. Motorcycle posts were also established for emergency work. At no time did it become necessary to employ runners except in the most forward areas during an engagement. The work of First Lieutenant Paul S. Edwards, Signal Corps, and his small group of Signal Corps enlisted men, in keeping communications open, was highly commendable.

Spirit

The spirit shown by officers and enlisted men of the brigade showed but little variation throughout the entire offensive. The spirit was splendid, and at all times showed a desire to cooperate wherever possible.

Medical Detachments

Medical detachments, under the command of First Lieutenant Alphonso Isom and First Lieutenant Louis Howard, did splendid work at all times.

Engagements

Eighteen separate and distinct engagements were fought by the brigade or elements of the brigade during the time covered by this report. This does not include the numerous times the Tanks were ordered out on wild goose chases, or the times they were required to follow in support.

In addition to these engagements, the 14th and 17th Groups (French Tanks) fought one action, directed against CHARPENTRY, independent of American Tanks. During their other engagements they operated with American Tanks, and their engagements are included in the 18 actions mentioned above.

During the period covered by this report, the Tanks cooperated with two Army corps and eight divisions, as follows:

    1st Army Corps
    5th Army Corps
    1st Division
    2nd Division
    28th Division
    35th Division
    42nd Division
    77th Division
    82nd Division
    91st Division

                SERENO E. BRETT
                Major, Tank Corps.

Casualties September 26 – November 10, 1918

Date	Officers Killed	Officers Wounded	Men Killed	Men Wounded	Total
Sept. 26	1	5	0	4	10
27	0	1	4	3	8
28	0	6	5	30	41
29	0	0	1	4	5
30	0	0	0	0	00
Oct. 1	0	0	3	13	16
2	0	0	0	12	12
3	0	0	0	1	.1
4	1	2	2	66	11
5	1	1	0	26	28
6	0	2	1	13	16
7	0	0	0	4	4
8	0	0	0	8	8
10	0	1	0	2	3
15	0	2	0	2	4
17	0	0	0	1	1
18	0	0	0	1	1
Nov. 1	0	1	0	1	2
Totals	3	21	16	131	171

Percentage of officers killed   5.34%
Percentage of officers wounded   37.5%
Percentage of men killed   2.33%
Percentage of men wounded   18.8%

A large number of men were evacuated on account of an epidemic of the "Flu".

TANK CASUALTIES

Tanks employed in the MEUSE-ARGONNE offensive   141
Tanks repaired for all causes   174
Percentage of tanks out of action for all causes   123.4%
Tanks demolished by enemy fire   18
Percentage of Tanks demolished by enemy fire   12.76%
Tanks missing in action   1
Percentage of tanks missing in action   .7 of 1%

These statistics are for the American Tanks only.

Image from Brett Report.

1st French Brigade at Meuse-Argonne

ARTILLERIE D'ASSAUT	With the Armies, 18 October 1918.
First Brigade
General Staff
No. 2666/0

Colonel Wahl, Commanding the First Brigade, A.S., to General Rockenbach, Commanding the Tank Corps, U.S.A.-

I have the honor of sending you two copies of my report on the operations of the French Tanks with the First American Army from the 17th of September to the 10th of October.

I have joined to the report some recommendations for decorations for some of the officers and enlisted men who particularly distinguished themselves in the course of these operations.

Colonel Wahl, Commanding the First Brigade, A.S.

(Signed) Wahl

OPERATIONS OF THE FRENCH TANK CORPS WITH THE FIRST AMERICAN ARMY

Artillerie D'Assaut, First Brigade, General Staff, No. 2631/0
From the 17th of September to the 10th of October,
Between the MEUSE and the ARGONNE.

SITUATION OF THE TANKS OF THE 1st ARMY THE 17th OF SEPTEMBER

After the operations of 12-16 September in the region of THIAUCOURT, the situation of the French Tanks with the First American Army was as follows:[44]

Groupments or Battalions.	Groupes or Companies		Number of tanks in fighting condition or susceptible of being put in fighting condition within 48 hours.		Locations.
505th Reg't.					
XIIIth Bn.	A.S.	337	21		)
	"	338	19		) Bois de la Cote en HAYE
	"	339	20		)
XIV Bn.	"	340	22		)
	"	341	21		) Bois de VILLERS-en-HAYE
	"	342	15		)
XVth Bn.	"	343	22		)
	"	344	23		) - d° -
	"	345	20		)
Groupment XI	"	34	11		) Bois de la QUEUE THENARD
	"	35	6		)
	SRR	105			Ferme NEYETTE (road from SAIZERAIS to LIVERDUN)
Groupment IV A.S.		14	C.L.	5	BERNECOURT
			Schn.	8	
	"	17	C.L.	3	- d° -
			Schn.	8	
	SRR	102			MESNIL-la-TOUR
S.P. 202					SAULX-enBARROIS
T.M. 70					- d° -

[44] Image from Wahl Report.

POSSIBILITIES OF USING TANKS IN AN OPERATION BETWEEN MEUSE AND ARGONNE

On September 4th the colonel commanding the 1st Brigade of Tanks was ordered by the general commanding the Tanks to have a reconnaissance made by the senior officer between the VERDUN-ETAIN ROAD and the eastern border of ARGONNE FOREST.

Commandant Chaubes, commanding the 502 Regiment Tanks, was selected. He made his reconnaissance September 5-7, and on the 8th sent his report to the general commanding the Tanks.

September 14th, General Rockenbach indicated to the colonel commanding the 1st Brigade the front of the contemplated attack. The colonel was then enabled to report to the general commanding the Tanks the following deductions:

A. Our first line is in the part obstructed by obstacles such as: the FORGES RIVER, MALANCOURT, CHEPPY, and MONTFAUCON WOODS. The enemy terrain is completely cut up by artillery fire to a depth of 4 to 5 kilometers. Generally speaking, the Tanks should not participate except north of the GERCOURT-CUISY-VERY line.

B. North of this line three openings offer favorable terrain for Tanks:

1. One opening running south north, 1 kilometer wide abreast of SEPTSARGES, and expanding to 5 kilometers north of NANTILLOIS.

2. One running southwest to northeast, west of MONTFAUCON and the ANDON RIVER (1000-1500 meters wide).

3. One zone bounded by the BUANTHE, the AIRE, the EXERMONT (rivulet), and the CHARPENTRY-ROMAGNE ROAD—meeting the aforementioned opening north of CIERGES WOODS.

September 17 the colonel commanding the 1st Brigade suggested the following distributions—which were adopted.

A. The 505 Regiment, comprising three battalions light Tanks and two groups St. Chamonds will operate:-

    1. Two battalions light Tanks and one group in the sector west of SEPTSARGES -NANTILLOIS.

    2. One battalion light Tanks and one group west of MONTFAUCON-GESNES.

B. Groupement IV—Schneiders—in sector north of BAULNY-CHARPENTRY.

September 22 a cipher telegram from GHQ placed the 17th Battalion Light Tanks (of the 506th Regiment) at the disposal of the 1st U.S. Army.[45] This battalion to be in reserve behind the elements of the 505 Regiment Tanks.

TRANSPORTING OF TANK UNITS TO ASSEMBLY POINT

The assembly point chosen for the Tanks was north of the STE. MENELHOULD-VERDUN ROAD between ARGONNE and NIXIEVILLE.

Groupement IV to take position in the eastern border of the ARGONNE near LOCHERES.

The light battalions and XI Groupement to take positions at CAMP CLAIRS CHENES (FAYS and SIVRY WOODS).

Entrainment - The economizing of trains was observed throughout. One battalion moved on two trains; the Groups 14 and 17 and the S.R.R. 102 moved on two trains.

Groupement IV entrained at ANSAUVILLE September 18: 1st train 5:00 p.m., 2nd train 11:00 p.m. Detrainment CLERMONT-EN-ARGONNE. Detrained September 21, assembly point LOCHERES.

XIII Battalion Light Tanks, entraining point VILLERS-EN-HAYE WOODS: 1st train 6:00 p.m., September 18, 2nd train midnight, September 19. Detrained September 21.

XIV Battalion Light Tanks, entraining point VILLERS-EN-HAYE WOODS: 1st train 6:00 p.m., September 19, 2nd train midnight September 20. Detrained September 22.

XV Battalion Light Tanks, entraining point VILLERS-EN-HAYE WOODS: 1st train, 7:00 p.m., September 20; 2nd train, 1:00 a.m., September 21. Detrainment September 23.

A.S. 34, Entraining Point RAPPE WOODS, 7:00 p.m., September 18. Detrained September 20.

---

[45] First Army.

A.S. 35, Entraining Point RAPPE WOODS, 7:00 p.m., September 19. Detrained September 21.

Detraining point DOMBASLE-EN-ARGONNE, assembly point, CLAIRS CHENES CAMP.

S.R.R. 105 entraining point PAGNY-SUR-MEUSE, 4:00 p.m., September 21. Detraining and assembly point SOUHESMES.

S.R.R. 102, which detrained at CLERMONT with Groupement IV, took position at CAMP FOURGOUS, east of the AUZEVILLE-BRAINCOURT ROAD.

XVII Battalion. Light Tanks at the disposal of the colonel commanding the French Tanks, and the 1st U.S. Army entrained at POIVRES, September 24: 1st train, 4:00 a.m., 2nd train 9:00 a.m. Detrained NIXIEVILLE the 25th, proceeding immediately to HESSE FOREST.

OPERATIONS FROM SEPTEMBER 26 – OCTOBER 3

General Conditions of the Operation

D-Day fixed for September 26.

Zero hour, 5:30 a.m.

IV Army[46] to attack in CHAMPAGNE.

1st U.S. Army to attack between the MEUSE and the eastern border of ARGONNE FOREST with three Army corps:-

3rd Army Corps[47] on the right.

5th Army Corps[48] in the center.

1st Army Corps[49] on the left.

The 5th Corps to attack in three divisions in line—from the right to left the 79th, 37th and 91st, the 32nd in reserve.

Disposition of the attack:

79th Division, 157th Brigade, leading, 158th Brigade, in reserve.

37th Division in each brigade, one battalion in line; the others organized in depth.

---

[46] Assume this is reference to the IV Corps.
[47] The III Corps.
[48] The V Corps.
[49] The I Corps.

The Tanks assigned to the 5th Army Corps, comprising the 13th, 14th, 15th, 17th Light Tank Battalions and the XI Groupement were placed under the orders of Commandant Mare commanding the 5th Regiment Tanks. The latter installed his command post at VILLE-SUR-COUSANCE.

The 1st Corps attacked in line with the 3rd.

The 35th was on the right.

Assignment of Tank Units to Large Units

The Tanks assigned to the 1st Corps, two light battalions of American Tanks and Groupement IV under command of Lieutenant Colonel Patton. The 35th Division attacked with brigades organized in depth; Groupement IV to support the two regiments on the right.

Plan of Attack for Tanks

<u>ZONE of 5th Corps:</u> The light battalions were attached as follows:
13th Battalion with the 37th Division.
14th Battalion with the 79th Division.
15th Battalion with the 79th Division.
17th Battalion in reserve for the Corps.
Groupement XI with the 79th Division.

It was arranged for the 15th Battalion to operate with the 4th Division — right division of the 3rd Corps.

On D-1 the Tank units were at their point of departure, northern point of GESNES WOODS.

At 0 hour the Tanks left this point to proceed to a rallying point north of MONTFAUCON WOODS. They were to reach this point at H plus 8. If the attack developed satisfactorily they were to be at the following points at H plus 12:

13th Battalion east of GESNES.
14th Battalion CUNEL WOODS.
15th Battalion BEUGE WOODS.
Groupement XI CUNEL WOODS.

If unsatisfactorily, the Tanks were to take orders—after H plus 8—for the divisions to which they were attached.

Preparations Necessary to Permit Tanks to Cross: the 1st American Position; the German Systems in MONTFAUCON WOOD

A path was to be made by the 37th and 79th Divisions as far as the northern border of MONTFAUCON WOODS.

For this purpose each division was to assign one Company Pioneers to the Tanks.

The work to be performed by the 79th Division was to be directed by Commandant Herlaut commanding Groupement XI; that to be done by the 37th, to be directed by Commandant Duclos commanding the 13th Battalion.

Liaison: The commanders of the light battalions [are] to accompany the generals commanding the divisions, company commanders with the brigade or regimental commanders.

Protective measures taken by Tanks: batteries were assigned to counter-battery fire on anti-Tank guns; the barrage to include a certain amount of smoke shells.

ZONE of 1st Corps: During the night of D-1—Groupement IV to proceed to point of departure west corner of COTES DE FORIMONT near the NEUVILLY-VARENNES ROAD.

At 0 hour the groups to leave the point of departure in column and in the following order:- A.S. 17, A.S. 14—to follow a course laid out in the itinerary—ravine west of BUZEMONT, western corner of ROSSIGNOL COMMUNICATION TRENCH CHEPPY, VERY.

In reality the groups were not to participate until reaching the Corps objective—VERY—a point to be attained at H plus 4:30. Nonetheless the captain commanding A.S. 17 was to accompany the colonel commanding the leading Infantry regiment, in order to call in his group if the Infantry were attacked.

Rallying point, west of VERY.

Preparations - A platoon and a half of American Pioneers was placed at the disposal of Groupement IV to complete the contemplated path, this to be?[50] Staff of the groupement. On reaching VERY the American Pioneers and accompanying Infantry were to be divided among the two groups.

Liaison - The commander of the group to establish his post of command at the following successive points:

The brigade over the BRANIERE RIVER.
The BITLIS SYSTEM.
The outlet north of CHEPPY.
The VERY MILL.

Protective Measure - One battery of the 209th Light Artillery selected for counter-battery fire on anti-Tank pieces.

September 26

<u>ZONE of 5th Corps:</u> The Tanks left their points of departure at 0 hour, but the work on the paths through the German lines progresses but slowly. The terrain was soggy and unfavorable, and instead of a Company of Pioneers each division sent but 100 men. At 1:00 p.m. the 13th Battalion, leading, was on a terrain a trifle more favorable, 400 meters south of CUISY WOODS. At this moment, the Infantry (79th Division) was stopped 200 meters south of CUISY WOODS by intense machine gun fire.

The captains commanding the 337th and 339th Companies were asked to intervene by the Infantry though this Infantry did not belong to the division to which the Tanks were attached—the 37th, two sections were engaged, and at 5:00 p.m. CUISY WOODS was cleared and delivered to the Infantry.

At 6:00 p.m. at the request of a colonel commanding the 313th Regiment Infantry, the commander of the 338th Company engaged one section against the woods bordering the MALANCOURT-MONTFAUCON ROAD. At the sight of the Tanks the enemy retreated and the woods were occupied by the Infantry.

At 7:00 p.m. the 339th Company engaged one section in the direction of MONTFAUCON and led the Infantry to the defenses south of there.

In leaving the path to aid the Infantry, the 13th Light Battalion left a number of Tanks behind. The splitting up of sections and the accompaniment of strange Infantry over a terrain that had never been reconnoitered was

---

[50] Word not legible.

patently contrary to regulations, but the Tanks nonetheless rendered great service. The Infantry, inexperienced and with little leadership, remained stationary. It was imperative that the Tanks should precede them in order to lead them forward.

Meanwhile, the 14th, 15th and 17th Light Battalions which had been delayed in MONTFAUCON WOODS awaiting the completion of the paths, began to arrive at the assembly point (northern border of CUISY WOODS) at 5:30 p.m.

Groupement XI did not reach the northern edge of MONTFAUCON WOODS until the morning of the 27th.

During the night of 26th-27th the four battalions (light) assembled in CUISY WOODS.

Throughout the day, the protective measures (artillery) were not able to function.

The congestion of the one-way road prevented the bringing up of smoke shells, and the batteries were not able to follow by reason of the soggy conditions and the blocking.

ZONE of 1st Corps: The two groups left the positions of departure at 0 hour and advanced along the path on which the work was progressing satisfactorily. The Infantry were stopped in front of CHEPPY and asked the aid of the Tanks. The 17th Battalion penetrated the village and encountered heavy resistance, the enemy using many anti-Tank rifles. At the entrance to the village the enemy machine guns allowed the Tanks to pass, thanks to the heavy fog, but the Infantry were held up. The 14th Battalion was then engaged.

The village was taken in the afternoon, and the Infantry supported by Tanks advanced beyond VERY. At the end of the day the groupement rallied west of the village.

Owing to severe losses in the 17th Battalion, the commander withdrew this battalion and assigned its available Tanks to the 14th.

September 27

<u>ZONE of 5th Corps:</u> The 13th Battalion was at the disposition of the 73rd Brigade (37th Division). The General in command of this brigade asked at 2:30 p.m. for one section to attack in the direction CIERGES. This section took up its position of departure but the order was countermanded. At 8:00 p.m. the section returned to the rallying point.

The commander of the 14th Battalion had the greatest difficulty in rejoining the commander of the brigade to which he was attached.

Meanwhile the commander of the 342nd Company, who had maintained liaison with the commander of the 313th Regiment Infantry, launched in concert with the latter a rapid attack with a view to encircling MONTFAUCON. MONTFAUCON was encircled. The Infantry did not follow but succeeded nonetheless in infiltrating into the village.

The 15th Light Battalion assigned the 343rd Company to the 314th Regiment. The 15th Light Battalion assigned the 344th Company to the 315th Regiment.

At 5:30 p.m. the sections preceding the Infantry cleaned up the terrain between MONTFAUCON east of SEPTSARGES, the southern edge of BEUGE WOODS and the ridge north of NANTILLOIS. The Infantry followed very badly and though NANTILLOIS was evacuated remained 1500 meters south.

The companies rallied at nightfall south of FAYEL WOODS.

<u>ZONE of 1st Corps:</u> The 14th Battalion supported an attack by the 140th Regiment Infantry on the CHARPENTRY-ROMAGNE ROAD.

The Tanks quickly reached their objectives in front of the Infantry who followed well. Two Tanks even reached CHARPENTRY but the Infantry organized their positions on the ridge southeast of the village.

September 28

<u>ZONE of 5th Corps:</u> The general commanding the division asked the commander of the 13th Battalion for three sections with which to support an attack by the 74th Brigade upon CIERGES.

Two sections were immediately sent to their positions of departure (85, 73) but the attack was put off till the morrow, the Infantry being unprepared. The sections remained at their positions of departure.

The commanders of the 340th and 341st Companies (14th Battalion) succeeded in finding the colonel of the 316th Regiment and offered him their services. The objective was very ill-defined—advance toward the north; first attack BEUGE WOODS. But there were no Germans in BEUGE WOODS.

There were some Americans south of WOOD 286. The Tanks cleared the edges west of WOOD 268 and 250 and reached MADELEINE WOODS, but though they returned several times to lead the Infantry forward, the latter recoiled before the artillery fire.

The 79th Division which had that morning taken BEUGE WOODS and the ridge north of NANTILLOIS received orders to continue the attack toward CUNEL and to reduce the woods on each side of the NANTILLOIS-CUNEL ROAD.

The 344th Company supported the advance of the 158th Brigade. They destroyed machine guns, and led Infantry to the attack on the wood south of CUNEL.

But the Tanks encountered heavy artillery fire. The Infantry stopped. The Tanks got orders to retire. Two received direct hits. The Infantry immediately left the conquered terrain.

Groupement XI comprising but four batteries of three Tanks, attacked simultaneously with two batteries to the east of the road and two to the west.

The Tanks destroyed numerous machine guns. Some reached PUNALS[51] FARM and MADELEINE FARM, but the Infantry did not pass 268. The Tanks withdrew to TUILERIE WOODS and on the 29th to the north of MONTFAUCON WOODS.

ZONE of 1st Corps: The 14th Battalion, reconstructed with one battery of three Schneiders and with three Renault Tanks, was placed at the disposal of the 137th Regiment Infantry to continue the attack on CHARPENTRY-BAULNY. The Tanks led the Infantry two kilometers beyond the objective to CHAUDRON FARM.

---

[51] Spelled "Punais" in "Operations of the French Tanks-Execution" of the main report.

September 29

ZONE of 5th Corps: The three sections of the 13th Battalion awaiting at their positions of departure since the day before were placed at the disposal of the 148th Regiment Infantry to attack CIERGES. The sections went into action between ANDON and EMONT WOODS. No resistance developed at first, but from CIERGES on the heavy machine gun fire stopped the Infantry. One section advanced toward the village. The Infantry retreated, abandoning the Tanks. The two remaining sections withdrew but the section which had proceeded toward CUNEL did not return.

The 14th Battalion took position for an attack which was countermanded September 30.

The 15th Battalion placed the 344th Company at the disposal of the 138th Brigade to re-undertake its attack of the day before. The Tanks reduced MADELEINE FARM and OGNON WOODS. The Infantry followed only as far as OGNON WOODS. The Tanks were withdrawn at 6:00 p.m.; five Tanks were broken down in our lines, one of them struck by a shell. During the night the Infantry withdrew 1,500 meters in the face of light bombardment, leaving five Tanks (the broken down ones) and two which had remained on the terrain from the day before, in the enemy's hands.

ZONE of 1st Corps: Groupement IV was withdrawn and sent to LOCHERES.

September 30 - October 3

The Americans carried out the reliefs of the various divisions and their establishment in positions.

Unfortunately orders and counter-orders necessitated the units changing positions for the attacks which were revoked every day. The 14th Battalion suffered especially from these movements.

October 3, the 13th and 14th Battalions were withdrawn to HESSE FOREST.

Operations from October 4 - 10
General Conditions of the Operations; Method of Using Tanks

After a period of reorganization and reliefs, the 5th U.S. Army Corps was to affect a joint attack with the 3rd U.S. Army Corps.

The 32nd Division replaced the 37th. The 3rd replaced the 79th. The boundaries of the 5th and 3rd Corps were slightly modified.

October 2, Groupement XI was placed at the disposal of the 3rd Corps and specifically with the 4th Division Infantry, the left-hand division. But on October 3 upon reaching the post of command of the 4th Division, Commander Herlaut learned that the sector of the 4th Division had been taken over during the night of October 3-4 by the 80th Division, and vice versa. This relief hindered a great deal the establishment of liaison which had been completely affected with the 4th Division.

<u>3rd U.S. Army Corps:</u> The 80th Division to attack in depth, the regiments in line in the brigade; in each regiment the battalions in depth.

The groupement was reorganized into a scratch group of four batteries, three of them containing four Tanks each, and one of them containing three.

One battery was attached to the assaulting battalion on the right. The other two (of four Tanks each) were assigned to the assaulting battalion of the left. The three-Tank battery was to support the supporting battalion—as a cleaning up battery.

Objective: PULTIERE WOODS – north of CUNEL.

<u>5th U.S. Army Corps:</u> The 15th Light Battalion was attached to 3rd Division. The 17th Light Battalion was attached to the 32nd Division. The disposition of troops in the 3rd Division to be the same as in the 80th.

The 343rd Company (2 sections) attached to battalion assaulting on the right; the 344th (3 sections) to that on the left. The 345th Company (1 section) to the supporting battalion on the left.

Objective: ROMAGNE-CUNEL.

The evening of October 2, the 32nd Division changed its order of attack. It was decided to attack with brigades in line instead of in depth.

The 17th Light Battalion gave one Company to each brigade. The 3rd Company was held in reserve.

Objectives: the heights north of GESNES.

D-Day fixed for October 4, 0 hour, 5:25 a.m.

October 4

ZONE of 3rd Army Corps: The Group XI attacked with three batteries of three Tanks each, the fourth battery having been broken up to complete the attacking batteries.

At first the attack proceeded normally with the Tanks leading. Then it stopped south of OGNON WOODS. The Tanks cleared the borders of OGNON WOODS along the southern edge, called the Infantry, and returned several times to find them. About 11:00 a.m. the Tanks were caught in a heavy artillery fire and being unable to persuade the Infantry to leave the WILPRE SPRINGS RAVINE, withdrew.

ZONE of 5th Army Corps: The Tanks cleared the banks east of the ANDON, the western borders of CUNEL WOODS, and attacked CUNEL and ROMAGNE. The Infantry followed well, took NAMELLE TRENCH, and organized on the EAST-WEST ROAD, about 300 meters to the north. Owing to severe losses they remained on this line.

Many Tanks were held fast in the swampy banks of the rivulets that cut this terrain.

During the night the Infantry abandoned a part of its gains.

The 15th Light Battalion was withdrawn and rejoined the other Tanks October 6 at CAMP CLAIRS CHENES.

As the 32nd Division had not attacked at 0 hour owing to being unprepared, the Tanks went to the rear.

At 4:00 p.m. the attack was resumed. The Tanks advanced as far as GESNES, but the Infantry did not follow.

October 5

ZONE of 3rd Army Corps: At 11:30 p.m. October 4, the 3rd Corps decided to resume the attack to the north of WILPRE SPRINGS. A scratch battery of four Tanks was organized. It was agreed with the colonel commanding the 318th Infantry that the Tanks were to lead at 100 meters and would return to fetch the Infantry if it did not follow.

The attack was launched at 10:20 a.m. At 10:35 the Infantry had ceased following the Tanks. The only Tank in running order, retired. At 3:00 p.m. October 5 the general commanding the 3rd Corps released Groupement XI.

The six and seven remaining Tanks retired to SIVRY WOODS.

ZONE of the 5th Army Corps: The 32nd Division decided to resume the attack that had broken down the day before. Two sections of the 17th Battalion were engaged. This time the Infantry followed and the Tanks cleared GESNES, the woods to the east, HILL 235, and MARINE and CHENE-SEC WOODS.

October 9

ZONE of 5th Army Corps: The 17th Light Battalion received orders to assemble at CAMP POMMIERS near RECICOURT with a view to being subsequently employed. Nevertheless, the 351st Company was left at the disposal of the 32nd Division to take part in an attack that had been prepared the 7th and 8th by reconnaissance.

Objectives: ROMAGNE and the heights to the west.

The 32nd Division had one brigade in line, the regiments arranged side by side. Each regiment had two battalions in the first line.

One section was assigned to each of the attacking battalions; one section in reserve.

Axis of attack: CIERGES-ROMAGNE ROAD.

One section to the east; one to the west.

0 hour fixed for 8:30 a.m. but at the order of the general commanding the 63rd Brigade, the Tanks left alone at 11:00 p.m. They passed the Infantry at NAMELLE TRENCH and one supported the attack on ROMAGNE which was taken.

At 4:00 p.m. the 341st Company was released.

October 10 the 17th Light Battalion was assembled at POMMIERS CAMP.

REGROUPING AND WITHDRAWAL OF TANK UNITS

The regrouping of Groupement IV and the 13th and 14th Light Battalions was ordered October 1, 1918. Groupement XI and the 15th and 17th Light Battalions alone remained at the disposal of the attacking units.

The movement commenced the next day. The 13th and 14th Light Battalions went to HESSE FOREST.

Groupement IV having been definitely retired from the battle entrained October 5 at DOMBASLE-EN-ARGONNE and detrained the 6th at POIVRES. The S.R.R. 102 was left where it was to take care of salvage.

By cipher telegram 4015/m October 6, the General Commander in Chief ordered the 13th, 14th, 15th, 17th Light Battalions and Groupement XI to rest in the VERDUN-AUBREVILLE region with a view to further operations.

The entraining orders arrived the 8th and were executed as follows:

13th Light Battalion entrained in two trains at SOUHESMES-LA-GRANDE on the 10th.
14th Light Battalion in two trains at SOUHESMES-LA-GRANDE on the 11th.
15th Light Battalion in two trains at SOUHESMES-LA-GRANDE on the 12th.

Owing to lack of railroad material Groupement XI was unable to entrain the appointed day— October 12—and was forced to await the arrival of material. By a change in cipher telegram 4015/M the colonel commanding the 1st Tank Brigade received orders to place a unit of the 17th Light Battalion at the disposal of the 17th Army Corps with a view to operating on the right bank of the MEUSE.

Consequently one Company (20 Tanks) was transported by tractors of Motor Transport 70 during the day of October 12 to the east of the MEUSE.

The departure of the battalion was deferred until the company detached from the 17th Light Battalion had been withdrawn from the battle.

WIRELESS TANKS

Only the light battalions were equipped with wireless Tanks. These took practically no part in the action, since all of the divisions and brigades did not possess the 10 BIS apparatus, and those that did have them did not want to use them. On the other hand, ignorance of the English language hindered the radio operators a great deal.

The commander of the 14th Light Battalion used his Tanks for liaison with the rear of his battalion. One Tank remained with him; another followed the companies.

In the 15th Light Battalion one Tank stayed with the Infantry brigade, another with the regiment. One message sent by the colonel of the 316th Regiment was very disappointing. The antenna was often laid bare and the antenna holder broken if the guide rope was allowed to trail. It is difficult to protect the radio apparatus from dampness.

Some breakage in the fan belts laid up the Tanks for a rather long time; the replacement of the reservoirs having not yet been made.

GERMAN ANTI-TANK DEFENSE

Nothing new to announce.

The active defense played no great part except in the sector of the 1st U.S. Army Corps (active defense-rifles and cannon). It seems that the village of CHEPPY which was filled with anti-Tank defenses is an example of the anti-Tank force announced in a recent bulletin.

The turret of one Renault was struck straight on by an anti-Tank rifle bullet and perforated. A metal scale the size of a five franc piece was detached from the inner wall.

In the 1st U.S. Army Corps zone there were many mine fields, but the placards "ACHTUNG MINENFELD" which the Germans had forgotten to remove, enabled us to avoid these dangerous spots. Nevertheless one Tank blew up.

TACTICAL CONCLUSIONS

On the greater part of the attacking from [sic] the Tanks supported an Infantry which not only knew nothing of fighting with Tanks but what is more had never been under fire and were not skilled in Infantry combat.

Groupement IV supported by the 35th Division which had seen some experience obtained good results. October 4th, 14th Battalion attacked with the 3rd Division which had already seen action. Here again the ground won by the Tanks was occupied.

September 26 the attack enjoyed a partial success. The forward movement being stopped the effort immediately dwindled. No orders were forthcoming and the Tanks in order to keep busy reduced to participating in minor operations until September 29. Even these minor operations were often suggested by the commanders of the battalions or the companies. Sometimes the Tanks would lead the Infantry forward. From September 27-29 the battle was conducted by the Tank staff.

The 4th, 5th, and 9th of October the American command succeeded in giving an impetus to the whole. The results were much better and the gains realized were partially taken advantage of by the Infantry's occupation.

TECHNICAL CONCLUSIONS

St. Chamonds

Most of the damage was damage to tracks, derailments, breakage of the attaching caps of connecting rods on forward chariot and breakage of male and female hinges. It seems that the successive reinforcements of these parts have been insufficient remedies.

The adoption of a rigid track might solve this question and so relieve the workmen and crews of the arduous and discouraging labor necessitated by these incessant repairs.

Schneiders

The Schneider Tanks have been so thoroughly used up as to make it impossible for them to go into action. The motors have lost part of their power and the friction has so increased that these Tanks are powerless in front of the slightest obstacle. It was necessary for the crews to perform marvels to attain the results they did.

Renaults

Breakdown of two kinds—the second being in part the result of the first:

a. Breakage of fan belts and fan belt pins.
b. Fusion of piston rod heads causing breaking of piston rod heads and the breaking of the crank case by the piston rod.

It seems it would be possible to diminish the breaking of fan belts and fan belt pins:

a. By placing the two ventilator pulleys in the same plane.
b. By governing down the motors the 1,500 revolutings—the speed beyond which there is considerable slack in the side of the fan belt which is not on tension.
c. By equipping the battalions and the park sections or repair sections with indicators permitting them to ascertain the maximum revolutions the motors are capable of attaining.

The best solution would be to replace the belts by gears. The fusion of the piston rod heads is in great part caused by the breaking of the fan belt or the fan belt pins, since this brings about the overheating of the motor—which in an inexperienced driver may not be noticed in time.

Besides, the Tanks have no method, while they are in motion, of controlling the circulation of oil. A pressure gauge attached to the oiling system would permit control at all times.

It is frequently impossible to start the Tank from the inside. An electric starting device would have many advantages, noticeably a decided saving of gasoline.

The light Tanks made by Herliet occasion the following remarks: for the first 100 hours, perfect; thereafter a rapid and general wearing out of all parts. This is probably caused by the poor quality of raw materials employed.

The behavior of the Schneider-built Renaults was satisfactory.

Wheel Vehicles

The operations between the MEUSE and ARGONNE bring about the same conclusions as those of the ST. MIHIEL.

Of the two-ton Renault trucks, five were patently weak.

It would be better to equip the light Tank companies and heavy groups with five five-ton trucks, the battalion and groupement staffs with two powerful motorcycles and side cars, the regimental staff with a touring car, a small truck, and an extra motorcycle.

The brigade staff has equal need of a small two-passenger car for long distance liaison (of daily occurrence) or at least another motorcycle.

Repairs

The ordinary repairs were made by the echelons and the S.R.R. 102 and 105. The more important repairs were made by the mobile units of the section from Park 202 at WALY (this refers to repairs on Renaults). The Renaults were taken on Latil tractors belonging to Motor Transport Company.

AS 202 served as Park Annex to P.A.S. and to Auto Bailly DE BAR-LE-DUC.

Gasoline supply was difficult on the battlefield. The congestion and disorder of the roads forebade the use of motor vehicles.

The 505th Regiment was forced to call on pack mules, each one carrying 100 to 150 litres of gasoline. This ingenious solution cannot always be used. It is to be hoped that two or three Schneiders (lightened) may be attached for supplying each battalion or groupement in the line.

Salvage and Repair

The extrication of Tanks left on the field by the 505th Regiment and 18th Battalion was effected by AS 102 aided by four Schneider Tanks of Groupement IV, two of which had been lightened and two made over into platform Tanks. Five Latil tractors and trailers also took part in the work.

The extrication progresses under good conditions. The Tanks were assembled at DOMBASLE-EN-ARGONNE station. Some were sent over the G.P.A.S. to BOURRON and some by F.A.S.2 to MAILLY-POIVRES.

(Signed) Commander of First Brigade Tank Wahl
Sept. 1 – Oct. 12, 1918.

Losses in Materiel from September 26th to October 10th.

Groupments an Battalions	Groups and Companies	Tanks fit for action Sept. 25th	TANKS Hit by shell	TANKS Hit by mines	Tanks left on field In our lines	Tanks left on field In their lines	TANKS fit for action
505th Regt.				October 7th, 1918.			
13th Battalion	337 Co. 338 Co. 339 Co.	21 19 20	11		16	9	4
14th Battalion	340 Co. 341 Co. 342 Co.	22 21 19	8		15	3	27
15th Battalion	343 Co. 344 Co. 345 Co.	22 22 20		1	8	10	2
			October 10th, 1918.				
17th Battalion	349 Co. 350 Co. 351 Co.	15 18 15	2		16		32
			October 7th, 1918.				
Groupment XI	34 Co. 35 Co.	11 5	2		3		3
			October 8th, 1918.				
Groupment IV	14 Co. 17 Co.	6 L.T. 16 Sch.	2 Sch	1 Sch	1 L.T. 5 Sch		3 L.T.

Image from Wahl Report.

Losses in Personnel from 17 September to 12 October 1918.

Groupments and Battalions	Groupes and Companies	Officers Killed	Officers Wounded	Officers Missing	Enlisted Men Killed	Enlisted Men Wounded	Enlisted Men Missing	Total
13° Bn.	A.S. 337					1		1
	" 338		1			6	3	10
	" 339		1		2	4	6	13
14° Bn.	" 340				1			1
	" 341				1	7		8
	" 342					2		2
15° Bn.	" 343		1		1	9		11
	" 344			1	3	9	2	15
	" 345		2			6	3	11
17° Bn.	" 349					5	6	11
	" 350				1	3		4
	" 351				1	5		6
Groupment XI	" 34)	1	5		3	14		23
	" 35)							
	Inf.d'acc.					4		4
	SRR 105							0
Groupment IV	A.S. 14		2			8		10
	" 17		3		6	16		25
	Inf.d'acc.		1			10	1	12
	SRR 102							0
Totals		1	16	1	19	109	21	167

Image from Wahl Report.

Gasoline and Ammunition Consumed.

Groupments or Battalions	Groups or Companies	Number of Engagements	Gasoline consumed from the departure from the Rendezvous until return to the overhaul park.	Machine gun belts fired	Shells fired
505 Regiment:					
XIII° Bn.	A.S. 337			30	
	" 338	2	21,500	40	1480
	" 339			30	
XIV° Bn.	" 340			48	
	" 341	2	28,000	64	1681
	" 342			9	
XV° Bn.	" 343			65	
	" 344	3	32,000	53	2040
	" 345			60	
XVII° Bn.	" 349				
	" 350	3	36,000	26	2340
	" 351				
Groupment XI	" 34	3	5,550	271	571-75'
	" 35	3			
Groupment IV	" 14	3	1,430	180	(350-75'
	" 17	1	1,090	182	(200-37'
					(231-75'
					(137-37'
Totals		16	125,570	1058	1152-75'
					7878-37'

Image from Wahl Report.

301st Battalion with the British Expeditionary Forces

2nd Tank Brigade, American Expeditionary Forces
Report on Operations: September 27th – October 1st, 1918

Reference Maps:
1/20,000 WIANCOURT; 1/40,000 Sheet 62c and 1/40,000 Sheet 57c[52]

"Z" Day – September 29th; Zero Hour – 5:50 a.m.

(1) GENERAL PLAN.

The 4th Tank Brigade, consisting of:-

> 1st Tank Battalion, B.E.F.
> 4th Tank Battalion, B.E.F.
> 301st Tank Battalion, A.E.F.
> 4th Tank Supply Company, B.E.F.

was allotted to the Australian Corps, whose front is shown on the attached maps.[53]

The II American Corps,[54] affiliated with the Australian Corps were to attack in the general direction GOUY-NAUROY at 5:50 September 29th.

The American Corps was to attack with two divisions (27th on the left, 30th on the right) in the sectors shown on the map attached hereto.

After the penetration of the HINDENBURG LINE the divisions were to push on to the first objective indicated by the green line, east of the sector GOUY-NAUROY.

If the objective had been taken by the 27th and 30th Divisions, the 3rd Australian Division on the left and the 5th Australian Division on the right were to pass through the front line American divisions and capture the second objective indicated by the red line.

---

[52] Only one map included with archived Report, "The Le Catelet-Bony Offensive." Its image is included with this transcription.
[53] Not included. See footnote 51.
[54] II Corps.

The preliminary bombardment was to last for considerable period. The 18th British Division on the left of the 27th Division was to attack simultaneously as far as the canal.

The operation was divided into two phases, the boundaries and objectives being shown on the accompanying map. The American Corps was to complete the first phase, the Australians the second phase.

First Phase

The 54th Infantry Brigade (U.S.) with part of the 53rd Infantry Brigade following in rear of its left flank was to form up on a taped line prior to Zero Hour and with Tanks, were to attack under a creeping shrapnel, H.E.[55] and 10% to 15% smoke barrage.

On the map the start line is shown in brown and the objective in a continuous green line.

Upon gaining their objective, the Infantry were to exploit their success to the flanks under the concealment of a flanking smoke barrage.

Second Phase

The 3rd Australian Division with its own artillery and Tanks were to pass through the 54th Infantry Brigade in open warfare formation at Zero-5. Their objective is shown in red on the map.

In order to secure the left flank of the operation, and extend the base of the salient thus created, reserve troops of the 27th Division were to extend their operations to the north and secure the objective shown in red on the map.

Tanks

301st Battalion was allotted to the 27th Division:
    "A" Company - 15 Tanks to 108th Infantry.
    "B" Company - 10 Tanks to 105th Infantry.
    "C" Company - 15 Tanks to 107th Infantry.

---

[55] High Explosives.

Remaining seven Tanks were held in Australian Corps reserve.

1st Tank Battalion, British, allotted to 30th Division.

(2) PRELIMINARY PREPARATION.

At a conference on the morning of September 19th the G.O.C. 4th Tank Brigade informed commanding officer of 301st Battalion of the general plan, at a conference held at 301st Battalion Headquarters, which was also attended by company commanders. All reconnaissance officers were directed to prepare maps and obtain information of the operation area at once.

The time available for training with Infantry was very curtailed and no arrangements were made. The 27th Division had a limited amount of training with British Tanks before arrival in the Australian Corps area.

On the morning of September 20th all Tanks of the battalion were fit for action, though wooden spuds and cribs had not been issued. Cribs were attached on the afternoon of X-Day and spuds on Y-Day (for Mark V Tanks only).

(3) RECONNAISSANCE.

General

As in other operations where surprise was the main factor, time for reconnaissance of the area was very limited. Reconnaissance started a week before the attack.

As soon as it was known that the 301st Battalion was to cooperate with the 27th Division, the plan of the attack was communicated to company commanders and reconnaissance officers.

Reconnaissance officers prepared the route to the lying-up point and the starting point. The selection of the lying-up point and the rallying point was made by brigade headquarters.

Aeroplane photographs were carefully studied and all the obstacles, trenches and enemy works discernable were noted on a record map which [was] kept by battalion reconnaissance officer. All intelligence information was transferred to this map.

Layered route maps were prepared for each battalion, company, platoon, and Tank commander. Oblique photographs of the sector and a map showing his route, obstacles, etc., were given to the Tank commanders 24 hours before the attack. In conference with the Tank commanders, each company reconnaissance officer gave them all the information it was possible for him to obtain. One of the company reconnaissance officers made a set of notes for each Tank commander in his company, describing his particular route and the landmarks, etc., he would find on it.

In this connection it is strongly urged that in actions in the future more information be given to the Tank commanders and every officer concerned as soon as it is available. Secrecy is most important, but the longer a Tank commander has time to think and thoroughly understand exactly what he is to do, the better he will do it. In the present instance officers of the battalion learned some of the details of the coming action from the Infantry men before they were allowed to be given any information by our commanders.

It is also strongly urged that the battalion reconnaissance officer whenever possible, attend conferences with their battalion commanders and that company reconnaissance officers attend the conferences where the company commanders are present. This plan had been generally adopted in the British Tank Corps and is absolutely the best means of giving the reconnaissance and intelligence departments or units first-hand information necessary for them to carry out their work with the fullest understanding of the operation. In addition the reconnaissance officer is present if he is needed to answer any questions which may arise.

The reconnaissance officer is concerned mainly with the routes from the starting point to the objectives. Nearly all his time prior to the action must be devoted to this work and imparting this information to the Tank commanders. As our organization does not provide for assistant reconnaissance officers, it is suggested that an officer from each company be detailed to reconnoiter and be responsible for area routes, i.e., routes from Tankadrome to lying-up points and starting points. This should be an officer capable of taking up the work of the reconnaissance officer should he be injured.

Two of our Tanks and several British Tanks were blown up by running over mines which had been laid by the British Forces last March just in front of the front line. The field extended across the front of Company "A"'s sector and no notification of its existence was received before the attack.

The routes to the approximate front line were taped by the reconnaissance officers on the north of our sector. The battalion reconnaissance officer and Company "A" reconnaissance officer were wounded and a Sergeant Draughtsman killed laying tape south of the sector and these Tanks were led over their routes to the jumping off point by a sergeant and corporal from the reconnaissance staff.

Each Tank commander took into action one ST. QUENTIN 1:10,000 Map, one VALENCIENNES 1:100,000 map, one WIANCOURT 1:20,000 map with routes, obstacles, barrage table and objectives drawn on it, and oblique photograph of his sector. In addition to this a 1:20,000 layered map was given to each Tank commander to study the day before the engagement. Company "C" Tank commanders also carried notes of their routes. These route maps, photographs, etc., were practically useless due to the indefinite starting point and the thickness of the smoke. In the future it is advised that the Tank commanders be given a 1:20,000 map of their sector to study at least four days before the attack.

One Tank commander from each platoon was taken over the route from the lying point to a point as near as possible to our front line. Observation from here was very poor, but under any condition in the future it is recommended that each Tank commander be taken as far forward as possible some days before the engagement and everything which can be seen pointed out to him.

Reconnaissance within Our Lines

At the time the first information of the operation was received the battalion Tankadrome was located 25 miles from the operation area. Section and Tank commanders were occupied in equipment and repair of their Tanks, so that the reconnaissance officers had to do most of the reconnaissance.

Pooling of Reconnaissance Officers

Prior to "Z" Day, company reconnaissance officers were withdrawn to battalion headquarters where they and their draughtsmen worked with the battalion R.C. in his reconnaissance office.

This method is considered to be satisfactory; it also saves much duplication of work and ensures the proper distribution of information.

Supply of Information

Maps were good and an abundant supply was available. The WIANCOURT 1:20,000 proved invaluable. In addition the barrage map was issued on the same sheet.

Oblique photos were in good supply and found of great value when visibility was possible. Copies of some of the oblique photos are attached.[56]

(4) <u>TANK EQUIPMENT.</u>

The battalion was equipped as follows with Tanks:

	Mk V Star Male	Mk V Star Female	Mk V Star Composite	Mk V Male	Mk V Female	Mk V Composite	TOTAL
Company A	9	2	4				15
Company B	7	2		3	1	3	16
Company C				7		9	16

Note:- All Mark V Tanks Carried Cribs.

Image from Sasse Report.

In addition one Renault Tank was issued to battalion headquarters, but due to a broken track shortly before the battle, it was never used.

---

[56] Not filed with Report stored at Carlisle Archives.

(5) PRELIMINARY MOVEMENT BY RAIL.

The battalion entrained at ACHIET-LE-GRAND (G.10 – central, sheet 57c) and detrained at EQUANCOURT (V.10 central, sheet 57c) as given in the following schedule.

Train No. 13 – 12 Tanks Company "A" at 1:00 p.m. September 21.
Train No. 14 – 3 Tanks Company "A" at 3:00 p.m. September 21.
              9 Tanks Company "B" at 3:00 p.m. September 21.
Train No. 16 – 7 Tanks Company "B" at 3:00 p.m. September 21.
              5 Tanks Company "C" at 1:00 p.m. September 22.
Train No. 17 – 11 Tanks Company "C" at 1:00 p.m. September 22.
              1 Tank Company "C" (Renault) at 3:00 p.m. September 22.

Ramps were provided at entraining and detraining points by railroad Engineers and marches to and from Tankadrome occurred without incident. In each case, detrainment at EQUANCOURT did not occur until after dusk.

The battalion established a Tankadrome at MANANCOURT MILL (V9, c and d., sheet 57c).

Motor transportation with supplies, rations, etc., traveled overland.

(6) FINAL ARRANGEMENTS.

At a conference on the afternoon of September 23rd, the G.O.C. 1st Tank Brigade gave final instructions to Commanding Officer, 301st Battalion for the operation. The 301st Battalion was allotted to the 27th Division A.E.F. of which 30 Tanks were to operate with the 53rd Infantry Brigade and 10 Tanks with the 105th Regiment. The battalion commanding officer was directed to confer at once with Commanding General, 27th Division and make detailed arrangements for the plan of attack, also to submit a plan showing routes to start line and rallying point selected.

Battalion commander conferred with Commanding General, 27th Division on the night of September 24th, and the allotment of Tanks was arranged as follows:

Company "A" 15 Tanks to 107th Infantry
Company "C" 15 Tanks to 108th Infantry
Company "B" 10 Tanks to 105th Infantry

The remaining seven Tanks were held in Australian Corps reserve. Due to the fact that the 27th Division had never had an actual operation with Tanks, the Infantry commanders did not seem to grasp the idea of Tanks cooperating with Infantry.

On September 25th a conference was held at Headquarters, 27th Division attended by all Tank officers down to and including section commanders. Upon completion of the conference they conferred with the Commanding General, 53rd Infantry Brigade and gained his approval of plan of operation as submitted by the battalion commander.

From September 25th until "Z" Day, company commanders and section commanders conferred daily with corresponding Infantry commanders. Final plan of operation shown on sheet attached.

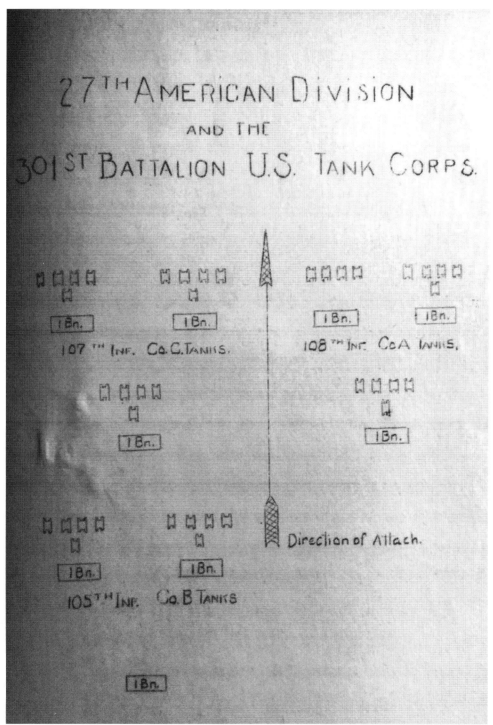

Image from Sasse Report.

One section of Tanks was to operate with each of the battalions of the 107th and 108th Infantry during the first phase, while two sections were to operate with the 105th Infantry during the second phase.

Arrangements were made with the Surgeon of 27th Division for evacuation of our wounded while Chief Engineer, 27th Division was requested to ramp a railway to be crossed during the approach march. The A.P.M. 27th Division was also notified of one road to be used on Y-Z night.

The 4th Tank Brigade assigned one wireless Tank to the battalion for the operation and issued orders that it was to follow between "A" and "C" Companies during the attack.

(7) APPROACH MARCHES.

To maintain surprise all movements took place under cover of darkness, and the approach, owing to numerous tracks existing, was simple and took place as follows.

27/28 September - 15 Tanks Company "A," 10 Tanks Company "B" and 15 Tanks Company "C" from MANANCOURT MILL (V9, c and d, sheet 57c) to vicinity of VILLERS FAUCON.

28/29 September - 15 Tanks Company "A," 10 Tanks Company "B" and 15 Tanks Company "C" from VILLERS-FAUCON (E21 b central, sheet 62c to start line – see WIANCOURT Map).

A supply dump had been established in the vicinity of VILLERS FAUCON by the brigade, and ten limbers were assigned to the battalion for hauling supplies from dump to the Tankadrome. On the afternoon of September 28th (Y Day) all Tanks were fully supplied with petrol oil and grease, and in addition carried one-half fill to be used at the start line before Zero.

The approach march on Y-Z night covered 8,500 yards, and Tanks left the half-way house at 10:00 p.m. This march occurred under very trying circumstances. The latter part of the route was constantly shelled by H.E. and gas shells, but fortunately only a few casualties occurred. One crew was slightly gassed, one Tank broke a track, and another stripped its gear. With the exception of Tanks as shown on the battlegraph sheet all Tanks crossed start line at Zero. Aeroplanes were to be employed to cover the final stage of the approach march, and down the noise of the engines. Only one aeroplane was heard during the entire march, and in several cases Tanks were halted for over one-half hour. However counter-battery work took place during the entire night and it is rather doubtful if the enemy heard Tank engines before Zero.

The original plan for the approach march on Y-Z night arranged for Tanks to leave half-way house at midnight. It is now conceded that had this plan been carried out, Tanks would not have crossed the line at Zero. On the afternoon of Y day the plan was altered so that Tanks left lying-up places at 10:00 p.m. All routes were taped from lying-up place to start line—a distance of about 3,000 yards.

Infantry guides met the reconnaissance officers of Company "C" and assisted in laying tape to our start line. Infantry guides were also arranged for Company "A" but did not appear. "B" Company used the same routes as "C" Company.

The taped routes were laid by reconnaissance officers and their assistants under very hazardous conditions, as it was afterwards learned that tape had been laid into the enemy lines. Two reconnaissance officers were wounded and one killed (sergeant) while laying tape.

Hot food was not provided for the men before the battle though arrangements for same were to be made.

With the exception of Tanks failing to start due to mechanical trouble, the remainder crossed the start line at Zero.

(8) <u>CONDITIONS.</u>

Weather

On "Z" Day a light mist covered all valleys in the area of operation which cleared at 7:00 a.m. The remainder of the day was fair and gave prospect of excellent cooperation with the Infantry.

Ground

On the whole, ground conditions were good and proved excellent going for Tanks.

One vital point of importance was neglected, though the fault was due to no one of the battalion. Previous to the German offensive during the spring of 1918, an anti-Tank mine was laid in the MAQUINCOURT VALLEY by the British forces as a defence against German Tanks. At the time of the operation on September 29th, no one in the battalion was notified that the mine field was in existence. It proved disastrous to two of our Tanks.

Several Tank commanders on the north sector report evidence of signaling from Infantry, machine gunners, and aeroplanes to enemy artillery relative to Tanks. It is quite evident that some system was used to inform the artillery of the location of Tanks as nearly every one drew a concentrated artillery fire.

One crew reported running out of six-pounder ammunition and one of running out of track oil after three or four hours fighting, though all drew their full quota before starting. Nearly all the crews were seriously hampered by lack of pistols and in some cases this resulted in men taken prisoners after having evacuated their Tanks.

Several Tanks signalled to the Infantry shortly after starting with good results. Flags were used for this. Pigeons were carried and could have been used to good advantage by several Tank commanders.

The greatest casualties to Tanks were caused by direct hits from artillery fire. Several Tanks were able to go on after being pierced in a number of places by armour piercing bullets and anti-Tank bullets.

Some mechanical defects developed during action. One Tank could not keep up its oil pressure, one stripped its gears, and several had auto-vac trouble. These Tanks were all able to get back to the starting point.

Stores were not removed in Tanks evacuated in our own territory but those evacuated in enemy territory had machine guns removed and the six-pounder disabled where possible.

The dump supply was very unsatisfactory, due to the fact that the rallying point selected was under heavy shell fire and machine gun fire and untenable for any length of time. It would have been much better had each company rallied separately behind their respective starting points.

Cribs were found unnecessary in most cases; all trenches including the Hindenburg Line being crossed without their use. The Tank which crossed the

ESCAUT RIVER at LE CATELET however used its crib and would not have been able to cross without it.

Nearly every man which took part in the action states that great benefit was derived from the ampules of ammonia furnished by the Medical Corps. These were constantly used and should be plentifully supplied in the future.

Tank commanders unite in the opinion that it was impossible to find their way about, pick targets, or work with any degree of effectiveness due to the thickness of the smoke barrage. The wind from the northeast blew the smoke back and enveloped the Tanks with the result that in some cases drivers could not even see the horns of their Tanks and it was impossible to see what they were running into.

Though all Mark V Tanks were equipped with cribs, none were used to cross the Hindenburg Line, as the latter in this particular sector proved to be no obstacle for heavy Tanks.

(9) <u>OPERATION.</u>

On September [sic][57] a preliminary attack by the 106th Infantry in the sector held by the 27th Division failed to establish the brown dotted lines as shown on the map attached. Plans for the operation for September 29th were only changed to the extent that the attacking units of the 27th Division were to advance at such time before Zero that would ensure placing them on the dotted line at Zero. The tactical officer with the 301st Battalion discussed this particular phase of the operation with the Commanding Officer, 107th Infantry at 5:00 a.m. on "Z" Day and was informed by the latter that the 107th Infantry would not leave their present position (approximately 1000 yards west of start line) until Zero. During the entire operation this particular unit was far behind its protective barrage and never gained contact with Tanks or Infantry on either flank.

Tanks of the 301st Battalion went forward in accordance with the original plan, "A" Company cooperation [sic] with 108th Infantry though "C"

---

[57] Day left blank but according to another source, it was September 27. Charles Bean, <u>The Australian Imperial Force in France during the Allied Offensive, 1918</u> (Canberra, Australian Capital Territory: Australian War Memorial, 1942), pp. 952, 953.

Company never gained contact with Infantry to which they were attached. "B" Company followed until Tanks were knocked out.

From Zero until 3:00 a.m. the wind was favorable and carried all smoke into enemy lines. For the remainder of the morning until 10:30 the entire battlefield was covered by a dense smoke created by our own barrage. Tanks could not see Infantry or vice versa. Most of the Tanks receiving direct hits were placed out of action by 8:00 a.m. previous to change to an unfavorable wind.

No difficulty was experienced in crossing trenches where it was possible to see. In cases where Tanks were ditched in trenches and sunken roads, the smoke was so thick that it was impossible to see the ground. The ground crossed was all good for Tanks and would have offered no obstacles. In a few cases ditched Tanks were dug out with shovels. One Tank was unditched by stretching a wire cable across two opposite spuds on each track. Other badly ditched Tanks were evacuated.

It was impossible to recognize any point on the ground due to the thickness of the smoke barrage. Tanks lost their way almost immediately after leaving the tape and had nothing to depend on but their compass. Nearly every Tank commander declared his compass invaluable and those who had defective compasses report that their lack of them was a serious handicap.

A number of crews report difficulty with Hotchkiss guns and bolts. No difficulty with the six-pounder is reported.

Nearly every Tank drew concentrated artillery fire. A great deal of this seemed to come from the neighborhood of RICHMOND QUARRY. It has since been established that one enemy battery remained at RICHMOND QUARRY all of "Z" Day. Armour piercing bullets and anti-Tank were extensively used and two Tanks were hit by British six-pounder shells coming from the direction of GILLEMENT FARM. One Tank commander reported an "Anti-Tank Fort" in LE CATELET and another reported the injury to conning tower by a grenade or bomb. No pits or Tank traps were encountered except the land mines previously referred to.

Crews were very exhausted after three or four hours fighting due to the long approach march and effects of gas.

The morale of the personnel of the Tanks Corps was excellent. In a dense smoke barrage it was necessary for someone to lead the Tanks over difficult ground and invariably [it was] the Tank commander. Crews went forward with machine guns after evacuating Tanks. Infantry Commanders with whom Tanks cooperate expressed themselves in high terms to the part played by Tanks throughout the battle.

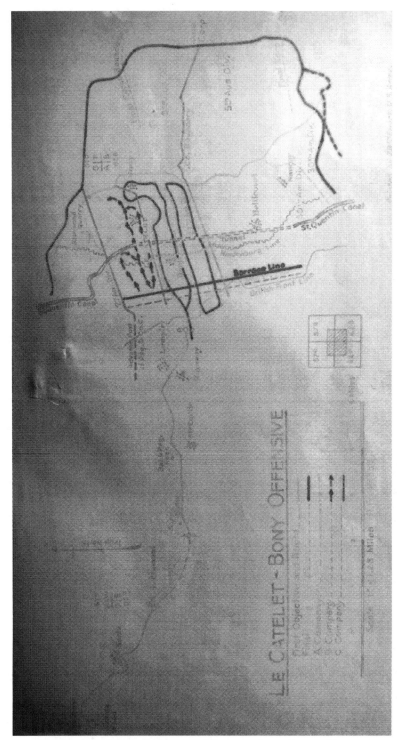

"Le Catelet-Bony Offensive." Image from Sasse Report.

The attack was unsuccessful

At the end of "Z" Day, the line had advanced in the sector of the 30th Division to the green line, while the 27th Division reached MAQUINCOURT TRENCH (A.2.c.2.3. WIANCOURT), BONY (A.15.a.central) and (A.27.b.9.9).

Failure can be attributed to the following:

(a) Insufficient counter-battery work.
(b) Failure of the 107th Infantry to advance at the proper time.
(c) Failure of Infantry to mop up in rear of firing line.
(d) Unfavorable wind for smoke barrage.
(e) Failure of Tanks to cooperate with Infantry.
(f) Failure to obtain a definite start line for Tanks and Infantry.

10. <u>COMMUNICATIONS.</u>

(a) Telephone
(b) Wireless
(c) Despatch Rider
(d) Aeroplanes
(e) Runners

No pigeons or mounted orderlies were used.

Telephone

Battalion headquarters at ST. EMILE (E.24.central, sheet 62c) was in connection with 4th Tank Brigade Headquarters at TEMPLEUX-LA-FOSSE.

Wireless

One wireless Tank was assigned to the battalion and followed immediately in rear of "A" and "C" Companies. Communication was established with brigade headquarters.

Despatch Riders

Two despatch riders were stationed at battalion headquarters and eight at brigade headquarters.

Aeroplanes

Dropping stations were located at battalion and brigade headquarters. Battalions must lay their strips carefully on the ground and have a man permanently detailed to look out for messages.

Runners

Each company commander had two runners, while several were stationed at battalion headquarters.

Due to the smoke barrage observers were unable to use the attack of either Tanks or Infantry, and very few messages were sent. It is believed that the operation was not a fair test of any system of communication.

(11) TACTICS.

In preparation for the operation, Tank tactics were based upon tactics for heavy Tanks as employed by the British Tank Corps. Without a barrage Tanks are deployed in depth and with a barrage Tanks keep close to the barrage. At the present time, the British use four Tanks per action, while Tables of Organization for American Tank Corps give five per section. The Commanding Officer, 301st Battalion decided that for this operation, with the barrage he would use four Tanks close up to the barrage, with one Tank in reserve, maintaining the section of five Tanks.

As the advanced Tanks were rather limited, it is thought that the plan was not given a fair trial, as the success of the operation involved a number of other factors.

(12) SUPPLY.

Eight Tanks of the 4th Tank Supply Company were allotted to the 301st Battalion. All supply Tanks were loaded with four fills of petrol, oil and grease, three fills of water, one fill of S.A.A., one-half fill of six-pounder and one-half fill of six-pounder case shot.

Supply Tanks moved with battalion during approach marches and came under command of battalion commander at 12 noon X-Day. Supply Tanks dumped their fills at the battalion rallying point.

In addition, ten horse limbers were allotted to the battalion for hauling from dump to Tankadrome. This method of transportation is considered invaluable.

(13) ARTILLERY.

The program for bombardments before Zero Hour were as follows:

Gas from Z-56 hours to Z-48 hours. Vigorous counter-battery work from Z-48 to Zero. Intense harassing fire from Z-48 to Zero. Cutting lines and hostile wire from Z-48 to Zero. The barrage came down on the artillery start line at Zero. Rate of barrage was 100 yards every four minutes. There was a halt for 15 minutes on the line approximately 500 yards east of the Cans [sic]. Final protective barrage at the end of the Field Artillery barrage continued for 15 minutes. (Time shown on barrage table attached is not correct).[58]

(14) SALVAGE OF TANK EQUIPMENT.

Unfortunately the battalion did not start to salvage equipment from derelict Tanks as soon as practical after the operation, although ten horse limbers were at their disposal. Derelict Tanks on a battlefield are subject to marauding parties of all kinds and valuable instruments are liable to be lost. It is suggested that in any future operation, salvage of Tanks commence as soon as possible upon the completion of the operation.

(15) ANTI-TANK DEFENSE.

It was evident in this operation that the enemy had been giving a good deal of consideration to the question of anti-Tank defense. The principle types employed in their order of damage to Tanks were:

---

[58] Table not included with archived Report.

(a) Field and anti-Tank guns firing over open sights at any Tank target.
(b) Anti-Tank Rifles. These were used extensively but it is only where the men have been trained in their use that they are really dangerous. Several were found lying about the battlefield.
(c) Armour Piercing Bullets. All Tanks gave evidence to the fact that a great number of armour piercing bullets were fired during the operation as the sides of Tanks had been punctured in many places, resulting in several casualties to personnel.
(d) Stockades, deep holes, cutting or anti-Tank aircraft were not encountered.

(16) <u>LESSONS AND SUGGESTIONS.</u>

Tactical

The necessity of smoke protection for Tanks operating in daylight was conclusively proved, though smoke created by an artillery barrage when blown up on advancing forces creates disorganization, loss of direction, and lack of cooperation between Tanks and Infantry. It is strongly recommended that all Tanks be equipped with Commander Brock's smoke device,[59] enabling a smoke barrage to be created at will. In the meantime, proper use of smoke bombs will afford a certain amount of protection.

There was a marked tendency on the part of some Tank commanders to get too far ahead of the Infantry and consequently to lose touch. Crews must be made to realize that the object of Tanks is to get the Infantry to its objective. [If] an Infantry cannot get forward owing to opposition, the first duty of the Tank is to overcome that opposition. To do this it will be necessary for Tanks to come back to their Infantry and to lead them forward again. In any case, touch must not be lost.

In dealing with villages or localities comprising a series of dugouts, sufficient Infantry must be detailed for mopping up purposes. Tanks cannot clear dugouts. This was demonstrated throughout the front of the 27th Division. In several cases the enemy kept reappearing from dugouts which had not been mopped up after Tanks had passed them.

---

[59] Frank Arthur Brock. https://en.wikipedia.org/wiki/Frank_Arthur_Brock

Tank commanders must be made to realize the importance of using local ground cover and of avoiding sky lines.

Training

Previous training should always take place between Infantry and Tanks before the operation. Infantry who have been trained with Tanks take advantage of fleeting opportunities created by the Tanks.

Compasses in all Tanks have proved their value. Too much cannot be laid upon proper training with the compass.

The use of smoke grenades from Tanks needs much practice and training before becoming practicable in action.

Technical

All officers of the battalion concede that the Mark V Star Tank is underpowered. Valve adjustment must be very carefully watched as well as the auto-vac system. As most of our Tanks are new, and the battalion had spent nearly three weeks in overhauling them and repairing them for action, only minor mechanical trouble was encountered.

Bullet splash is very bad, except at the flanges where the angle iron affords protection. Anti-Tank rifle fire and armour piercing bullets appear to necessitate the provision of thicker armour, at least in belts; that is to say on the horns, but [sic] around the vital parts of the machine.

Increased speed and power of machines will be the chief factor in overcoming anti-Tank rifle fire and armour piercing bullets.

General

Horse transport (limber wagons) proved to be essential. They should reach the battalion by Y-Day at the latest.

More light transport is required by the battalion during operation for company and section commanders to liaise with the Infantry units. Battalions often have to operate with two or more divisions and the distance between the various headquarters is great.

It is further suggested that the Tank Corps should have their own pigeons. While no pigeons were used in the present operation it is believed that they are a valuable means of communication.

<u>A Tank Unit to be successful must have intensive training by night and day, both with and without Gas Respirators.</u>

<u>I believe in Esprit de Corps.</u>

R. I. Sasse
Major, Tank Corps
Tactical Officer

301st LOSSES IN ACTION ON SEPTEMBER 29

HEADQUARTERS 301st CENTER, TANK CORPS.
AMERICAN E.F., ENGLAND.

October 8th, 1918.

From: Commanding Officer
To: Chief of Tank Corps, American E.F., France.
Subject: Report of action and casualty list.

    1. Following informal report on the 301st Battalion and casualty list received from my tactical officer this date. Am forwarding them to you as I do not know whether they have already been sent to you.

    2. This in my opinion emphasizes the point made by me in my letters to you of recent date as to the advisability of maintaining a training center here where facilities are at hand for heavy Tank training.

    3. At present, if the 303rd Battalion is kept intact, I have 15 officers of all ranks and 20 enlisted men that are trained suitably for any future replacements that may be needed in the 301st Battalion.

H. E. MITCHELL,
Lieutenant Colonel, T.C.

HQRS. 2ND TANK BRIGADE, AMERICAN E.F.,
Attached 4th Tank Brigade, B.E.F.,
September 30, 1918.

Lieutenant Colonel H. E. Mitchell,
Headquarters American Troops,
Worget Camp, Wareham, England.

My dear Colonel Mitchell:

    The Battalion went into action at 5:50 a.m. September 29th, co-operating with the 27th Division, A.E.F. Forty Tanks were supposed to cross the line and at the present writing it is believed that only thirty four actually started. Due to terrific anti-Tank defense, Tanks as well as infantry never reached their final objective.

Lieutenants McKay and O'Kane were killed and Captain Varney and ten lieutenants wounded. Twenty-one other ranks were killed, sixty wounded and <u>approximately</u> fifty men are either casualties or missing.

All Tank commanders state that they inflicted heavy losses on the enemy and that opposition was exceedingly great. Anti-Tank guns and anti-Tank rifles were thick in this particular sector. In addition one mine field had to be crossed. One Tank in command of Lieutenant Dunning crossed the Hindenburg line and the canal and into the village of Catelet, passed beyond and attempted to take what is since believed to be an anti-Tank concrete fort. They were put out of action and the Tank commander with the entire crew remained behind the enemy's lines until dusk and he, with one sergeant, succeeded in reaching our lines.

The morale of the battalion is excellent, but due to bitter fighting they seem somewhat shaken and need pulling together.

During the night of the approach march we were constantly shelled by both gas and H.E. which necessitated wearing gas masks most of the way.

While laying tape, Lieutenant McCluskey and Lieutenant Naedele were wounded, the former rather seriously. Many of the Tanks were put out of action in the vicinity of the starting line, while others received heavy anti-Tank gun and rifle fire in practically every part of the sector.

Cases occurred where Tanks after being hit were evacuated by the crews who went forward ahead of the infantry with their machine guns or fought their way through the enemy's lines back to our troops.

We are waiting word to go into action again at any moment and I consider the replacements called for as rather urgent.

> Sincerely yours,
> R. I. Sasse,
> Major, U.S. Tank Corps.

Hqrs. 2nd Tank Brigade, American E.F.
Attached 4th Tank Brigade, B.E.F.
October 2, 1918.

From: Tactical Officer.
To: Commanding Officer, 2nd Tank Brigade, A.E.F.
Subject: Report of Casualties.

1. Report the following casualties in action September 29, 1918.

KILLED.

Second Lieutenant O. O'Kane
" " John D. McKay
Sergeant Doyle (1780043) Martin J.
" Dunkerly (1779979) Meredith L.
" Mapes (125247) Mervin E.
Corporal Anderson (1803353) Paul C.
" Calico (1803599) Jesse B.
" Hartzell (1776113) Calvin F.
Private First Class Howell (1803688) R. H.
" " " Kaemerer (1803692) George H.
" " " McMahon (1803477) Valentine C.
Private Hart (1803420) Harry A.
" Hasse (139809) Leo C.
" Weigland (1788854) Walter J.

WOUNDED.

Captain Kit R. Varney (since reported killed)
First Lieutenant Sibley B. McCluskey
Second Lieutenant Harold R. Dean
" " Joseph J. Gutkowski
" " Morton B. Hillsley
" " Henry A. Hobbs
" " LeRoy Mitchell
" " Hannibal E. Potter

WOUNDED (Continued).

Sergeant Bingham (1795173) Thomas H.
" Bradbury (1803794) Samuel
" Brown (135214) Wallace E.
" Cosgrove (1803796) Raleigh J.
" Coyle (1803797) Ambrose A.
" Follette (1803799) Hugh C.
" Jasper (1803573) Ira
" Kaufman (1803575) Charles E.
" King (1803814) Thomas H.
" Lacasse (134807) Leo
" Plagemann (1776060) Fred W.
" Ruhs (1803587) Henry M.
" Whitlow (1803553) John D.
" Williams (672401) Frank J.
" Woolford (1777031) John W.
Corporal Allen (1581550) Ben
" Chapman (1794521) John A.
" Crain (1803814) John C.
" Dielmann (1572393) Lawrence F.
" Hengst (1786559) Perry R.
" Kelchner (1776233) Earl Y.
" Reed (1827036) Samuel S.
" Schobel (1803625) Joseph E.
" Smith (1783230) Roy A.
" Wallace (1782098) William R.
" Witherspoon (1795803) Edwin H.
Private First Class Campbell (1803378) William F.
"   "   " Cox (1803671) George W.
"   "   " Davis (1776335) Russell C.
"   "   " Herron (1785493) James E.
"   "   " Hull (1803689) Walter N.

WOUNDED (Continued).

Private First Class Lanning (1783135) Enoch (should be Ray T.)[60]
" " " Leslie (1803451) Howard C.
" " " Moore (1803700) Clifford B.
" " " Rishel (1803513) Clarence
" " " Sanders (1789450) Enoch H.
" " " Unger (1787549) Charles S.
" " " Webb (1803722) Harrison W.

Private Barum (1847871) George W.
" Cahill (1788845) Thomas J.
" Goodwin (1848048) John
" Greer (1803625) Walter W.
" Hughes (1786630) Wayne W.
" Kakaletres (1803437) John
" Parkhill (1787549) Thomas H.
" Quarles (1803512) Lowry C.
" Scanlon (1788843) Jeremiah E.
" Shields (1038130) Cornelius
" Silver (1782758) Millard F.
" Turek (2353145) James F
" Waters (1779837) Herbert F.
" Welker (1783443) Chris.
" Williams (1787640) William
" Wingate (1787642) George M.

SLIGHTLY WOUNDED.

First Lieutenant Rosborough, William McK.
Second Lieutenant Earl B. Dunning
" " Albert H. Hilliard
" " Theodore C. Naedele

---

[60] Correction as it appears in the original document.

SLIGHTLY WOUNDED (Continued).

Second Lieutenant Richard A. Parks
    "   "   Charles R. Shanks
    "   "   Hugh S? Taylor.[61]
    "   "   Robert O. Vernon
Sergeant Anderson (254412) Beverly C.
    "   Berbling (1803637) Joseph F.
    "   Rosenhager (1803592) Carl E.
    "   Shipp (259953) Clarence C.
    "   Sky (2030085) Bernard
    "   Weisbecker (1803593) Harry E.
Corporal Coble (1803569) Larry
    "   Morton (1803616) John
    "   Sawyers (1803626) James
Private First Class Cooper (1784349) William J.
    "   "   "   Lonz (1803695) Clarence A.
    "   "   "   McGowan (1786870) Paul B.
Private Jones (1803757) James
    "   Kelly (1786695) Peter F.
    "   Shreve (1803779) John D.

MISSING BELIEVED PRISONERS.

Sergeant Barnard (1803596) Walter W.
Corporal Capstick (1803600) Richard J.
    "   Gagnon (1803603) Lewis P.
Private First Class Dailey (1803643) James W.
    "   "   "   Mohler (1803768) Ed R.
Private Adams (1785927) Charles R.
    "   Evans (137878) John R.

---

[61] Question mark and period in original document.

WOUNDED.

Cook Martin (1788759) Joseph E.

LATE REPORTED KILLED.

Corporal Rauf (1803621) Leo G.
Private First Class Green (640034) Potter
    "   "   "   McCain (1803655) Harold K.
    "   "   "   Sumner (1803718) Max M.
    "   "   "   Weber (1803723) Peter M.

                                R. I. SASSE, MAJOR T.C.

NOTE: [62]

    The attached list is correct to midday October second. However, while doubtful reports have been received that Captain Varney was seen at a First Aid Station, it cannot be authenticated.

    Lieutenant Seddon is partially insane and at the present time is AWOL.

    Lieutenant Parke is also under observation for temporary insanity.

RIS/hj   R. I. SASSE,
                                      Major, T.C.

---

[62] This note was attached as the last page to the above list of casualties.

PERSHING COMMENDATION

GENERAL HEADQUARTERS
AMERICAN EXPEDITIONARY FORCES
OFFICE OF THE COMMANDER-IN-CHIEF

February 20, 1919

Brigadier General S. D. Rockenbach
Chief of Tank Corps,
A.E.F.

My dear General Rockenbach:-

Now that active operations have ceased and many of your personnel are returning home for an early separation from the service, I desire to express to you and through you to the officers and enlisted men of the Tank Corps, my appreciation of the work that the Corps has accomplished.

From the beginning its history it has been a consistent uphill fight for accomplishment against almost unsurmountable difficulties in the way of obtaining Tanks for training or for fighting. Due to untiring efforts, a certain limited number were finally obtained from our Allies, the Corps was recruited from the pick of the personnel of all arms of the service, Tank schools were started on a practical basis in France and England, and by the middle of summer the Corps took the field with several battalions. Its history in active operation, though short, is a bright and glorious one. In both the American offensive at St. Mihiel and Meuse-Argonne of the First American Army, it was of material assistance in the advance. In the breach of the Hindenburg line with the British near La Catelet it also won glory. The high percentage of casualties among officers and men tells the tale of splendid morale and gallantry in action of your personnel and of their unselfish devotion to duty.

It gives me great pleasure to thank all officers and enlisted men of the Tank Corps and, in the name of their comrades of the American Expeditionary Forces, to convey our appreciation and admiration of their splendid work and gallant record.

Sincerely yours,
John J. Pershing.

Other Publications from

DALE STREET BOOKS

Military Strategy, Tactics and Training

Battle of Booby's Bluffs is a blunt depiction of incompetence by some American Army officers in World War I, who were unable to adapt their old-fashioned tactics to the new weapons of modern war–tanks, machine guns, stokes mortars, and airplanes. Written in the dream-sequence style of the infantry classic, Defence of Duffer's Drift, the main character is a pompous know-it-all who relives the same dream over and over until by trial and error he learns how to keep his men alive and win on the modern battlefield. Written under the pseudonym Major Single List, the anonymous author had good reason to hide his identity, given the number of feathers his amusing but highly critical book likely ruffled.

Cavalry and Tanks in Future Wars is a collection of articles written by George S. Patton, in which he applies his diverse experiences as a cavalry officer chasing Pancho Villa on the Mexican Border and a tank commander on the battlefields in 1918 France to defend the continued relevance of cavalry and tanks in future wars.

Defence of Duffer's Drift, by Sir Ernest D. Swinton, is a classic in the art of infantry tactics and required reading at many Army schools.

Diary of the Instructor in Swordsmanship is the second training manual written by George S. Patton, Jr., to teach cavalry officers the proper saber tactics and techniques for mounted and dismounted engagements. His first training manual, Saber Exercise 1914, covers the general rules, while this second manual presents more detailed instruction.

In Defense of My Saber is a collection of articles written by George S. Patton, Jr. extolling the virtues of his redesigned cavalry saber. It begins in the glory days when his saber was embraced by the Army as standard issue. It ends with its ultimate decline into irrelevance after the Great War—and despite Patton's ardent pleas to the contrary.

Saber Exercise 1914, a training manual on the art of swordsmanship for cavalry officers, was written by George S. Patton, Jr. the year after the War Department approved his radical redesign of the cavalry saber. The redesign necessitated a fundamental change in mounted and dismounted saber work—all of which is explained in this manual.

World War I in Europe

Battle of the Meuse-Argonne from the German Perspective, by Major Hermann von Giehrl, is a German military analysis of the Battle of the Meuse-Argonne. In Major von Giehrl's eyes, the Americans and French are the enemy. But his writing is surprisingly free of nationalistic fervor. Instead he offers an objective view of the 42 days leading up to the German surrender, written by a soldier, not a politician or apologist. Von Giehrl is candid in his assessment of the effectiveness of the French and Germans, traumatized by four long years of the modern battlefield overwhelmed by tanks, aeroplanes, machine guns, mortars and gas. By contrast, his description of the naïve but strapping young Americans as they arrived on a ravaged continent not yet having learned to fear the horrors that awaited them is truly poignant.

War Diary 1918, by George S. Patton, Jr. and Ranulf Compton, is the verbatim transcript of the original—and only copies—of the handwritten daily diaries required by the War Department to be kept by all commanders during the Great War. It contains the complete and unedited entries for the 304th (1st Provisional) Tank Brigade of the American Expeditionary Forces, personally signed by Patton for each day's entry. It covers three critical months–from September when Patton's brigade was preparing to enter combat (first at the Battle of St. Mihiel and then the Meuse-Argonne Offensive) to the final days leading up to the Armistice in November. Also included is the War Diary kept by Captain Ranulf Compton, one of Patton's battalion commanders, who commanded the forwarded units of Patton's brigade after Patton was wounded. Captain Compton's diary entries begin in the middle of August, as his battalion prepares for combat and continues through October, offering a detailed and personal report of the Tank battles from the front lines. Together these diaries offer a unique view of the Tank Corps Brigade—and its forward units—in the critical months of the Great War, when our boys—and their tanks—turned the tide of history.

World War II in Europe

Campaign in Poland 1939 is a previously classified analysis by U.S. military strategists at the Department of Military Art and Engineering, United States Military Academy, detailing the "Polish Campaign" instigated by the German invasion in September 1939. Included are maps showing the troop movements and engagements over the course of the four-week conflict that ended with a conquered Poland.

German Fifth Column in Poland, by the Polish Ministry of Information, exposes the treachery of the German population living inside Polish borders but lending clandestine assistance to the invading German Army in September 1939.

German Occupation of Poland was published by the Polish Ministry of Foreign Affairs in the first years of the war. It exposed for the first time to the world community the dire conditions in Nazi-occupied Poland with detailed reports on the summary executions of civilians, eviction of Poles from their homes, the closing of schools, synagogues and universities and the forced relocation of Jews into ghettoes.

Mass Extermination of Jews in German-Occupied Poland was written by the Polish Ministry of Foreign Affairs as a plea to the world community to save Polish Jews from the Nazis.

Trying to Stop a War in 1939 details the earnest and increasingly frantic communications exchanged between the political and diplomatic representatives of Great Britain, Poland, Germany and Russia in the year leading up to the German invasion of Poland in September 1939. Originally published by the British Foreign Office as a testament to its extraordinary diplomatic efforts to rein in Hitler's territorial ambitions, this historically important collection of speeches, communiqués, cables, letters, messages and notes has been faithfully reproduced verbatim.

Should Great Britain Go to War--for Czechoslovakia? was written by the Slovak Council in 1937 as "an appeal to British common sense for the sake of World Peace."

Polish Literature

Pan Tadeusz, written by Adam Mickiewicz, is a sweeping ode to Polish history and heritage as seen through the eyes of two warring families and the lovers caught in the middle.

Amateur Radio

Popular series of "Quick Study" books to prepare for the exam at the three levels of Amateur Radio License:

Quick Study for Your Technician Class Amateur Radio License
Quick Study for Your General Class Amateur Radio License
Quick Study for Your Extra Class Amateur Radio License

Made in the USA
Lexington, KY
09 May 2018